LETCHWORTH REMEMBERED

LETCHWORTH REMEMBERED

Memories of the Garden City
1939 - 1960

Edited and co-ordinated by
Heather Elliott and John Sanderson

EGON PUBLISHERS LTD

Frontispiece:	King George VI and Queen Elizabeth visit Letchworth in 1941.
Front and back endpapers:	Eastcheap at the 1953 Jubilee Trade Fair.
Half title:	W.H. Smith staff taking a break in 1952.
Title page:	Mollie Langford School of Dancing, 1949.
Imprint page:	Munts' exhibition stand at the Jubilee Trade Fair.
Contents page:	Preparing for a Round Table car rally.

Copyright © Egon Publishers Ltd 2001

ISBN 1 904160 51 4

Originated by Climacs Imagin, Letchworth
for Egon Publishers Ltd

Printed in England by
Streets Printers, Royston Road, Baldock, Herts SG7 6NW

All rights reserved. No part of this book may be reproduced or transmitted in any form or by any means, electronic or mechanical, including photocopying, recording or by any information storage or retrieval system without permission in writing from the publisher.

Contents

Acknowledgements		VI
Foreword		VII
Introduction		IX
1	War breaks out	11
2	The war at home	22
3	Evacuees	35
4	Letchworth under attack?	44
5	Life after the war	65
6	The town changes	82
7	Working in Letchworth	89
8	A town of bicycles	98
9	Garden City industry	100
10	Shopping	111
11	Organisations	119
12	Television comes to Letchworth	128
13	Leisure	134
14	Growing up in Letchworth	143
15	Schools	153

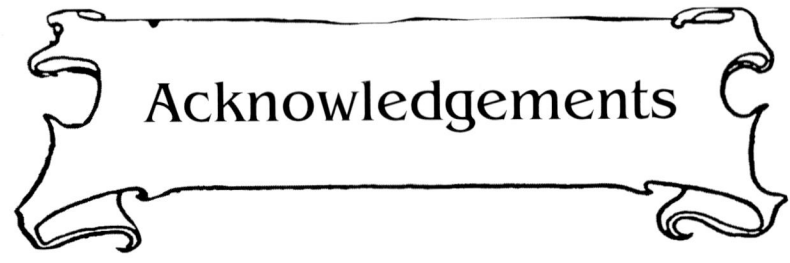
Acknowledgements

We should like to acknowledge the help and support given to us by the following, without whom this book would not have been possible.

Sheila Carrick, Suzanne Dorkacz, Heather Elliott, Will Farrier, Rodney Hall, Owen Hardisty, Pamela Haynes, Edna Imber, Melody Lucas, Vera Morley, Joan Walker, Andrew Miller, John Sanderson.

We should also like to thank the following people who were interviewed, provided written memories, loaned photographs or helped in some other way.

Ron Anderson, Mrs Joan Berrett, Mrs Margaret Bidwell, Mr Peter Billson, Mrs Audrey Bourne, Mrs Sheila Carrick, Mr G. D. Copeman, Mrs L. Corney, Mrs Jean Chalk, Pat Deans, Mrs Dulcea Ellis, Mr Will Fraser, Mrs P. Farrington, Mr Eric Fitton, Jack Gifford, Helen Gillespie, Mrs Rae Glenn, Mrs Sheila Hall, Mrs Sandra Hanley, Marion Hargraves, Mr Douglas Haynes, Mrs Greta Hewitt, Mr John Harper, Mr Ron Hope, Mrs Joy Howes, Mr Keith Howes, Mrs Edna Imber, Gladys Marston, Beryl Miles, Ruth Nunn, Mrs Brenda Overton, Margaret Pepper, Mr A. Peters, Mr Desmond Rix, Mrs Lesley Rolles, Mrs D. M. Scroggins, Mr Graham Seaton, Mrs Emily Sell, Mr Donald Senior, Brenda and Reg Smith, Mr John Smith, Irene Stacey, Mr John Stoddard, Daphne Sutcliffe, Joan Veazy, Mrs Joan Walker, Mr and Mrs Gordon and Joyce Wharton, Jean Williams, Mr Alan Wright.

We acknowledge the help and support of the Letchworth Garden City Heritage Foundation, the Letchworth Arts & Leisure Group and the staff of the Heritage Museum.

We would also like to thank Bletchley Park and the Tab Bombe rebuild project.

Whilst every effort has been made to credit all those who have provided information for this book, we regret any ommission that may have occurred.

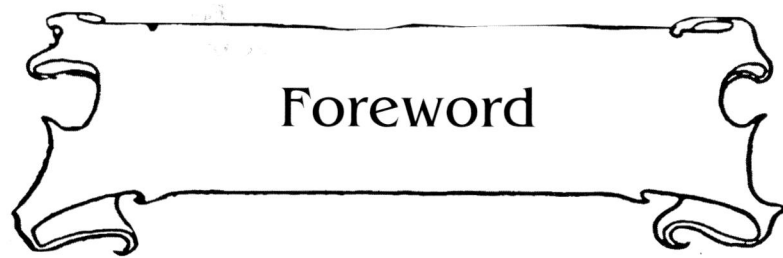

Foreword

No one has ever invited me to launch a ship. However, being asked to write a foreword may be rather like it, but this is as near as I have been, so far.

As I stand here aiming at the bows with this metaphorical bottle of dandelion and burdock from the Skittles Inn, I find that most of my life is passing before my eyes.

Possibly I am drowning, for Mrs Pooley never did succeed in persuading me across the outdoor swimming pool. No - this dazed feeling is due to the fact that I have just read right through this book, all at one go, unable (as they say) to put it down.

DON'T TRY THIS AT HOME. Take it one chapter at a time, and you'll love it. It is a warm pool of other people's memories, where you can paddle or float as you wish. Get your head under and you will hear the actual voices of real Letchworth Garden Citizens reliving events that - good grief, can't be as long ago as *that*, can they?

You will find yourself, like me, joining in and saying "Oh yes, that's right, I'd forgotten about that" - or sometimes "No, surely it wasn't" - although it probably *was* and you *had* forgotten.

For you kids not old enough to forget, this isn't just a book, but a time machine to take you to some of the strangest sights, from dried bananas in the Health Food Stores to milkmen's horses in Commerce Lane, and army tanks in Letchworth Gate. Oh yes, I remember them, when I blundered in along the lane from Willian, and the sentry at the barrier near the hospital turned round and said "Where'd *you* come from?" - but he let me go.

Obviously, World War II seems to occupy half of the memories here, though nobody had mentioned the colours of the buses. Our green Eastern National buses turned grey like battleships, and for a while they were joined by strange dark blue or maroon ones which were presumably evacuees from unknown boroughs in the Midlands. Why didn't I tell that to the editors when they asked for wartime memories? Or I could have confessed to my crime - throwing stones in the Emergency Static Water tank, where that futuristic Nexus building was going to be in the twenty first century. Perhaps the Special Constable who told me off is in the picture on page 14, which I had to turn over quickly.

In lots of the other pictures, you might find someone you knew, too, as I have just done. Like me, you may at last learn exactly why a thump on a television set made it work. I'd always wondered.

Old folk like me are supposed to say "I remember when this was all fields..." and thankfully in this book some of them do. Therefore as I fling this bottle at the bows, I name this book LETCHWORTH REMEMBERED, and good luck to all who have done it.

Come on, now, dive in and just listen to all these voices remembering!

KENNETH JOHNSON

A typical K.J. column from the pages of 'The Citizen'

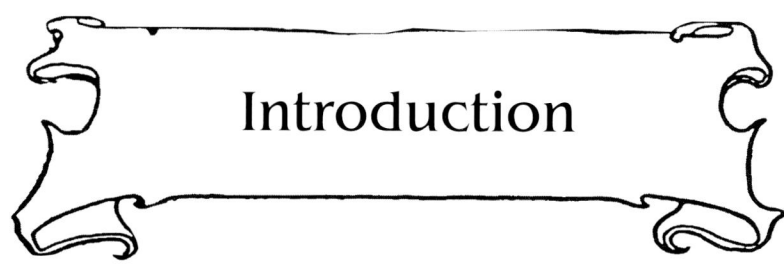

Introduction

Ebenezer Howard had a dream – build a garden city where people could live and bring up children in a clean healthy environment surrounded by trees and green spaces. He lived to see that dream made reality in Letchworth, the first Garden City. In 1995, a book called Letchworth Recollections was published, which recorded the memories of the first residents of this Garden City from the new town beginning in 1903 to the start of the Second World War. This book follows that with memories of the years 1939 to 1960.

It is a book of stories and anecdotes about Letchworth. In their own words, the people of the town recall their memories of life during that time. It starts with the war. Whilst Letchworth escaped with hardly any damage, there were plenty of incidents to remind the local population that they were at war. Diving into hedgerows as enemy fighters came over or spending the night in an air raid shelter in the garden are just some of the tales that are told. Letchworth was chosen as a safe haven for evacuees and there are many tales from evacuees and from those who took them in. The hardships of the war continued for some time afterwards, with rationing still in place. You will hear of the ingenuity of the locals and the steps they had to take to 'make do'. Letchworth's industry played a major part in people's lives and the stories tell of 'a town of bicycles' as everyone cycled to work in those days. After the war, Letchworth began to grow and people tell of living in the new estates. Finally, those who grew up in this New World tell their tales of play and schooling in the new Garden City.

This book has been complied by a dedicated team who have diligently recorded and transcribed interviews with all those willing to tell us their story. In the acknowledgements you will see names of those who have helped with this project.

This book in not intended to be a complete history of the time. We let the people of Letchworth know the project in local papers, magazines and at events and had a very good response with many people coming forward to tell their story. We even had a contribution from Australia. With such a wide cross section of people, we have covered many of the main aspects of Letchworth life during the period.

We have chosen to group similar items together and so some of the contributions will be split across different sections of the book. Whilst we have not been able to include everything that everyone told us, we have included sections from all the stories. As memories of events sometimes differ, we have chosen not to put names against individual memories, but to acknowledge all the contributions together. We would like to thank all those who came forward to tell us their stories.

As well as producing the book, the other aim of the project is to provide a rich resource for future research purposes and schools projects. All the tapes, transcripts and photographs will be lodged in the Letchworth Heritage Museum for future reference. It is also hoped that an electronic version of the material, and possibly a website containing the material, will be made available for schools and researchers.

We would like to thank many people and groups in Letchworth for their support and help in making this project work. Firstly we would like to thank all those who came forward and told us their stories and gave us a glimpse of what life was like during that period. Thanks are due to the interviewers and transcribers who spent may hours talking to the storytellers and then deciphering the contents of the tapes. The staff of the Heritage Museum provided us with assistance and with a 'dropping off' point for the delivery and collection of tapes and transcriptions. David's Bookshop and the Letchworth Arts & Leisure Group (LALG) helped with promotion of the project. We are indebted to Bob Lancaster, Curator of the Heritage Museum for his time in providing additional photographs for the book and for checking our draft copy.

Finally we would like to thank the Letchworth Garden City Heritage Foundation and staff for their support during the project.

Heather Elliott and John Sanderson

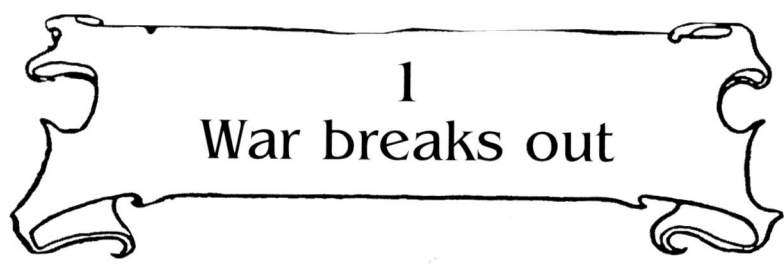

1
War breaks out

When war was declared on September 3rd 1939, the reaction in Letchworth was probably very similar to the reaction throughout the country. Letchworth residents remember the day very clearly, and one, at least, had a strange idea of what to expect!

At the end of the summer when my Mother told me that we were at war with Germany I rushed to the front gate being suitably impressed, and looked up and down the road expecting to see soldiers in armour on horseback.

My family was on holiday in Jersey in late August 1939 and we crossed the Channel to Weymouth as mines were being laid in its waters on the day before war was declared.

When war was declared on September 3rd 1939 I well remember sitting with my parents listening to Prime Minister Chamberlain's broadcast in such sombre tones. It was an emotional experience to know we were at war with Germany. We were living in a new house in Haselfoot (built by Bird and Sons the locally well-known family of builders). After the historic broadcast our new neighbours came round for a discussion, which centred round air raid precautions.

My first recollections of the War was the day War broke out and I was in my Guide uniform sitting in the Broadway Cinema waiting for a train load of evacuees to arrive when we were then asked to help with luggage and things, walking them to their respective destinations. I was at school at the time and the various preparations were made there. Everybody obviously was absolutely shattered at the outbreak of war and all sorts of preparations were made. All the windows along the corridors of school were taped over; there were sandbags around the doors and a row of cup hooks along the corridor from which one hung one's gas mask. When the siren went you had to go and stand by your gas mask in case it was required. This went on for some time but gradually, if you were really doing an exam or something, you didn't have to bother so it sort of petered out.

My father immediately became an ARP Warden and he took me with him around Spring Road and Sollershott when he was distributing gas masks. I had to show people how to put their chins in first and then pull on the mask. As I was only nine years old I really enjoyed helping him do this rather macabre job. Later he joined the National Fire Service and became a fireman by night and a printer by day. He was at the Garden City Press. He used to go to bed at home after a long day's work, for the young printers mostly had been called up. When there was a warning, as there were few private telephones in those days, a messenger on a bike would knock on our front door, call out "Red Alert", and then go on to the next man. Dad had to get up - pull on his uniform and run or cycle to the Area Fire Station at the junction of Spring Road and Icknield Way. This soon became too tiring and several men collapsed with fatigue so dormitories were built down there and a rota drawn up for all-night duties for the rest of the war.

Suddenly the sirens sounded for the first time. We than witnessed a spectacle I shall never forget. Our Air Raid Warden (newly appointed) appeared complete with his ARP equipment - a large tin hat a size too big and almost covering up his eyes, his armband, waterproof jacket, gas mask - and blowing his whistle. He ran up and down Haselfoot shouting 'take cover - take cover'. This brought all the neighbours out into their front gardens to witness this unusual event in an otherwise quiet Sunday tranquil setting! He urged the neighbours to take cover - but everyone was too intent gazing up into the sky looking for the bombers expected to appear at any minute.

The Warden instructed the neighbours who had been allocated fire-watch duties to produce their stirrup pumps, buckets of water and sand and to stand by for his further instructions. This the neighbours did - in great good humour! The Warden was so

Green Watch National Fire Service at G.C.A Office, August 1941

exhausted after his several runs up and down the hill that he dropped a bucket of sand on his foot. Surely one of Letchworth's first war casualties! My last memory that day was of him collapsed in a chair nursing his foot and surrounded by helpful neighbours all assuring him that the next time the siren sounds they really would take cover!

Air Raid Shelters

Air raid shelters were built in various places throughout the town to protect the residents at home, at work or on the streets.

I can remember diving into the air-raid shelters during the War. There was always somebody down there with a mouth organ or something to cheer the kids up so you couldn't hear what was going on outside if there was anything.

No one seems to know about the air raid shelter under Kennedy Gardens. I actually watched it being dug during my first visit here in the war years. I suppose I was about 11 or 12. I was in the town centre and I made my way to Kennedy Gardens. They had actually started doing it and being inquisitive to see how this thing was going to go, I was lying looking over the top and the next thing I knew I was in it. I went head over heels into this pit they were starting to dig. On the car park as it now is there used to be an ambulance parked. I can remember them getting me out of the hole, being carried into the ambulance. They cleaned me up and checked me out and kept me there for about an hour, but all I remember that I got from the fall was a bruised back.

There were air raid shelters in the Rose Gardens - Kennedy Gardens now. It was called the Town Square in those days. They are still there, I think, underneath the roses. Anybody shopping and caught in an air raid obviously went there. Not that, in fact, we did have that much bother with air raids but the siren did go very frequently.

Trenches were dug on the Arena - opposite the Council Offices. The Arena at that time was a square of grassland

My first job was with an evacuated firm from London, namely the Phoenix Book Company that were taking shelter within the offices of Dents, the publishers, in Dunham's Lane. When the sirens sounded we had to take shelter in the storage area where we were surrounded by shelves of books and paper. Taking shelter brings back a memory of the first time that we heard a siren at the very beginning of the war. We were in the Broadway Cinema watching a film with Joan Crawford starring when the siren sounded. As a body we all made for the shelters that were in the Arena, adjacent to the car park. We never did see the end of the film, and did not get our money back either.

LETCHWORTH COUNCIL

Black-out Offenders To Get Rude Awakening

POLICE TO TAKE ACTION

THAT the Letchworth A.R.P. Committee are not satisfied with the black-out in Letchworth was stated by the chairman (Mr. H. D. Clapham) in response to a question by Mr. R. W. Tabor at

Letchworth Special Constabulary

In Jackmans Place they were building the trenches and at the Ascot in Pixmore Avenue, the Government Training Centre there. All the trenches were dug in that lovely sports field there - long soft grass where the skylarks used to nest. It was a sports field but they never seemed to do much with it. Beautiful soft grass there. I suppose the trenches were to hide in - air raid trenches. I suppose they would have covered them over with shelters. There was a hostel there for people who came to the training centre. Then they rebuilt and trebled the size of the hostel and covered everything up, but it was where I seem to remember having my first cigarette, sitting under the planks in the trenches, puffing a bit of smoke and not feeling so good afterwards.

I remember going to the doctor's up the town - the Belgian doctor, Doctor Van Der Borght - and being ushered out of there and across the road to where the new telephone exchange is. There were air raid shelters there under the ground and that was the nearest one and we were ushered across and in there - on Bridge Road. I can remember the static water tanks being around, especially on sand pits.

During the war in the air raid shelters there was one in Burnell Rise between the trees. When the siren went we used to go in there.

Sometimes other strategies were in place for protection. People remember what used to happen when they went to school.

At Hillshott when there was an air raid warning we had to all wait downstairs. I had a small case with paper and pencil for games. Every day at home as it got dark you had to put blackout curtains on the windows so that no lights would shine.

We walked to and from Westbury School with our gas mask cases bouncing on our backs, passing the rather gloomy and smelly brick air raid shelter in Icknield Way. We were just glad that we did not ever need to take refuge there.

In 1939 I attended Westbury School and when the warning sounded we all marched - no running - to the four big air-raid shelters. They were where the school canteen is now. Mr. Boorer and the teachers kept our minds occupied by making us recite poems and times tables until the all clear.

I also remember after starting school in September 1944 - I went to Norton Road which was then primary as well as secondary - there were one or two occasions when we had to shelter in a corridor because of air raid warnings and possible attacks. This corridor was situated well inside the school away from open windows. I remember it was some 30 years afterwards when I went back to Norton in my role as a teacher, taking some children there, and came upon this corridor where we had sheltered and that certainly brought back memories.

Though fathers were away fighting in the services and we were always being reminded 'there's a war on, you know!' mostly it seemed rather distant to us children. We did have some practices at school to see how quickly we could put our gas masks on, and the whole school had to march out and go down into the air raid shelter which had been dug into the school field, to make sure we could all fit in. Gradually we got more careless about always carrying our gas masks and we had no more visits from enemy planes over Letchworth.

Letchworth Special Constabulary: Sgt. P. J. Tinkler receiving medal

School lessons were often interrupted by air raid warnings. We all walked to school complete with our gas masks in a box over our shoulders, and when the air raid siren went we hastily grabbed our school books and masks to take down the shelter. My gas mask was a Mickey Mouse one. I expect it was to make it more acceptable to a young child. The air raid shelter was next to the West View gate nearest the town, by the canteen. It always seemed ages before the all clear siren went, a long wailing sound, and then we could all come out again, It was a wonder and credit to the staff that our education didn't seem badly affected by all the disruption the war caused.

Many people dug shelters in their gardens – some not altogether successfully.

When Germany invaded Poland on Friday, 1st September 1939, my parents and I were just returning to Letchworth Station from a lovely week's holiday in Margate. I remember how grim the station looked with sandbags piled up against the walls to protect it from the blast of the bombs which we knew were already falling on Poland and would be our lot soon. My father had spent his 19th and 20th birthdays in the trenches in World War 1, so he was under no illusion as to what to expect. When we got home we dug a trench immediately in the back garden in Spring Road which soon acquired water in the bottom of it, so Mum and I declared we would take our chance in the cupboard under the stairs.

Together with a neighbour, Dad built a shelter at the edge of this land. I have a clear memory of one day, attending the first birthday party of David when the air raid siren sounded. We rushed for the shelter and on arriving and sitting in there we all remembered poor David still in his high chair in the house.

My father built an air raid shelter in our front garden and when air raids started we conscientiously tried to spend a night in it. Like a lot of people we found it so uncomfortable we soon gave this up and preferred to risk staying indoors and getting under the dining room table when we heard German bombers overhead. We learned to recognise the difference in the throbbing sound as they flew west towards the Midlands from the lighter, quicker tone on their return journey, their bomb load disposed of. Not much fell near us, we were mainly flown over, but I recall a "Molotov bread basket" making a great noise from the fields beyond the top of Bedford Road.

With memories of the first Great War our father dug an air raid shelter in our back garden and we spent our nights there when the air raid sirens went.

There were no air raid shelters at school but most people at home had air raid shelters put in their gardens, various sorts like Anderson.

My father was a builder so he had a huge air-raid shelter dug half in the ground. Consequently, it got exceedingly wet at the bottom. When the siren went, because my father was a builder, he was required to go to the Demolition Centre which was supposed to be in case of houses being destroyed or knocked down and getting people out and so on - the Rescue Service it was called. So our huge, well it seemed huge, air raid shelter at home was for my mother and I, my sister, our evacuee and my Grandfather who was elderly and infirm. My sister was two years old so my Mother looked after my Grandfather, I looked after my sister and our evacuee had to fill the bath in case the water mains were burst. That didn't last too long either because it was too wet and too cold and too horrible and we had underneath the stairs reinforced because that was supposed to be the strongest part of the house and the children slept there.

I also have memories of squadrons of planes always droning overhead and the air raid sirens often going off. I am sure it must only have been for practice because I can't remember ever going to a shelter. I can't remember where our local shelter would have been.

We used to have an air raid shelter in our garden. We used to go under the stairs, that was the safest place. We had everything there. We had a kettle in there. We used to spend hours and hours. You daren't come out. In those days everything was blacked out. We had curtains drawn. The cars had headlights with little tiny slits.

Anyway I can remember a lot about the War, because my husband and some friends built an air raid shelter. A few days later the police came to the door. They were looking for a big barn door that was missing from the farm, the old farm which wasn't in use. And when my husband came in for lunch I said to him the police have been round here looking for a door. He said 'Oh goodness, good job that's covered up. It's in the garden.' So I said 'Oh well, I didn't know anything about that'.

The Blackout

All over the country sirens were erected and the blackout was enforced. Letchworth was no exception. The town was very fortunate that no damage was caused to the town by bombing, but residents could see the flames as far away as London. It is perhaps surprising that Letchworth was not a target if you consider the factories in the town which were producing munitions, tanks, parachutes, etc.

The blackout didn't really bother me. When we first came home from hearing war had started, Mum and Dad were running around trying to black out all the windows and curtains. It was quite hilarious at times.

During the Blitz period we had many nights broken by air-raid warnings, but fortunately no bombs on Letchworth. In the blackout, however, we were able to see the red glow in the sky to the south where London was burning.

In 1939 when the War started the first thing we had to see about in the shop was the blackout. I remember that we had a wooden shutter affair which went round the door on which a black curtain was hung in front. All the windows inside had to be blacked out. It was funny to see people coming through this wooden partition pushing back the curtain and peering round and blinking in the light of the shop.

I got to be quite good, actually. I could see very well in the dark. I remember going out with a friend, and I marched her across the road (from the theatre it was) and she went sprawling. I could see the kerbs, but she did not see them, and she was so indignant with me because she tore her stockings, and they were on ration. I got used to being in the dark; perhaps it was the carrots I ate. I was very fond of carrots. Actually, your eyes got accustomed to it.

I remember blacking out all the windows and cycling everywhere with shaded bicycle lamps to get to evening classes.

In 1941 I think that's when the sirens were put up. One at the end of Bursland. When the sirens went, the first sign the enemy was coming over, there used to be a high pitched sound, up and down, up and down, and that went on for two or three minutes. The all clear one was a continuous sort of whistling noise sort of thing and when that died down we all came out from under the stairs, for that was where we used to go when the air raids were on and sit there until it was all over. There was complete blackout. Everybody had curtains to draw and no cars with lights on, complete blackout. So it was a bit dismal. That's how it had to be.

Letchworth Air Raid Wardens

Opposite the corner shop in Bedford Road, before the houses were built on the left-hand side going towards the Wilbury Road were a number of air raid shelters and on the opposite side were open fields where we used to play. From the top of Wilbury Hill by the Wilbury Hotel my father once showed me the terrible flames of London in the distance during the Blitz. He had woken me in the night and we had walked there to see "History." Like a terrible fireworks display under the searchlights. It was awesome.

The Home Guard

The men of Letchworth joined the Home Guard.

My husband was forced to go into the Home Guard. He couldn't go until I put his trousers right for him because he couldn't manage to put the things down over the boot, the putty bit.

During the war he was a special constable, and was the auxiliary driver. We had only one driver on the main police force. So when this policeman was off duty, my dad used to stand in and many a time he was fetched out at night to go off to do police duty. One particular time he had to go out to Offley where a bomb lorry and a petrol tanker had an accident and exploded and demolished a farmhouse at the top of Offley Hill.

I was born in June 1939 - 3 months before World War 2 broke out - so my memories of the early part of the War are totally non-existent, but I can certainly remember as I got a little bit older the Home Guard activities, particularly on a Sunday morning. There would be a file of them skulking by the hedge opposite where I lived and I can remember the leaves sticking out of the netting on the top of their helmets.

From time to time rumours would spread that the war would be over by Christmas, or by Easter, or mid summer, but come Christmas etc. nothing had changed and the fighting continued. The Home Guard went on manoeuvres after their day's work was done, but what they did and where they went was not revealed. I'm sure that they played a great part, and it was comforting to see them marching off to do their bit during those war time years.

The War outside Letchworth

Many men from Letchworth were, of course, called up to serve in the forces during the war.

I got called up at the beginning of 1944. I did six weeks training in the RAF. Then they wanted some good soldiers so they took half of us out of the Navy and half of us out of the Air Force and stuck us in the Army. I did my training in Northern Ireland at Ballykinler and while I

LATEST ADDITIONS TO LIST OF MEN IN FORCES

To Receive Christmas Cheer Parcels

IN addition to the list of men serving in the Forces to whom Christmas parcels will be sent by was at Ballykinla some of the wounded and walking wounded arrived over from Dunkirk so we had lots of talks with them. A little while later we were drafted and went over from Hull to Ostend.

Within a matter of six weeks from finishing my training and getting ready to go to the continent, I was in five or six different regiments. It was security. We left Hull to go to Ostend, after D Day and we went there and we joined the 7th Battalion Royal Welsh Fusiliers, 53rd Welsh Division, in the Ardennes in Belgium and then we went through parts of Germany and Holland.

Then the time came for me to join up. As it happened I would have been in the reserved occupation working for the Ministry of Health, as I did, because the post of billeting came under that. In order that I could join the forces, which I was determined to do, I had to volunteer before my actual date came up. So that I did. I left in October 1942 and joined the ATS - the Auxiliary Territorial Service. I was a member of the Personnel Selection Staff, which meant I had to travel all over the country. I met Letchworth people in various places. In fact one time I was stationed at Prestatyn in the Holiday Camp which was a Signals Training Centre. I bumped into the Minister from the Free Church who was visiting his son-in-law who was in the same camp. Also one of the officers there was a chap I had been to school with. Then after that, in 1944, I was sent to Belgium and there I met Ralph Nott who was one of the sons of Notts the Bakers - I already knew him. I was also lucky enough to meet a couple of Belgian sisters who had been at St. Francis' College before the War. I enjoyed, obviously, coming home on leave. During one of my leaves from Belgium I was at the Victory Ball and, quite out of the blue, I was asked to cut the Victory Cake on behalf of the service people. This was rather lovely for me as it did not feel like a service anyway. Also, at that particular time - that Christmas - I received a postal order from the people of Letchworth. There was obviously some sort of fund set up and I have got the actual bit of paper that came with it. It says "Good luck and best wishes for Christmas and the new year from all at Letchworth." It was the Christmas Fund for members of H.M. Forces and we received a postal order for ten shillings which was quite a lot at that time. The Chairman of the Fund was Fred Nott, the Appeal Secretary was Alfred Glennister and the General Secretary was F.C. Doyle and I think it was something to do with the British Legion so far as I can remember.

Those left at home were eager for news of what was happening at the front, and this came from a variety of sources.

The first we heard of actual fighting was the Battle of the River Plate where the German Battleship 'Graf Spee' was scuttled after being attacked by three of our cruisers. The chap who became my husband was involved in that and when he came back on leave there was great excitement about that. Also the 'Graf Spey' had on board some prisoners off the Merchant Ships that they had sunk. This was in the South Atlantic off Montevideo. One of the Merchant Navy Captains who was a prisoner on board the 'Graf Spee' was Captain Dove. His brother was the Roman Catholic Priest in Letchworth so we saw him too when he came home. Another person involved was Mr. Shapel whose wife was one of the people who came from Bexhill. He was on the 'Jarvis Bay' which was sunk. That was a very great tragedy to a very brave ship.

I spent four and a half years in the forces and I went all over. I remember when the Germans threatened to blow the Dutch dams. We were front line troops then and because the Dutch were starving they used to send ambulances through loaded with food and stuff like that. They came through our lines and on the way back they used to stop and have meals with us. I got talking to one fellow and it turned out eventually that he lived about 200 yards away from me. I still talk to him now.

I went to St. France's College where I stayed until the end of the War. Our Nuns were mostly Belgian and French so they - and we - followed the progress of the War with great interest and patriotism especially as three of the Nuns at the Mother-Convent in Belgium were in Gestapo Prisons for helping allied Airmen.

Embarkation leave

Sheila carries daddy's gas-mask,
Peter carries daddy's gun.
Mother's chattering on and laughing
As if parting were just fun.

War Weapons Week

War Weapons Week was held to raise money for the war effort. Letchworth raised an amazing amount, greatly exceeding its target.

The first such week was held in February 1941. I was asked to serve on the Savings Committee. Savings were a vital part of the Government's strategy to fund the war effort. Every factory had a savings group and all were encouraged to buy savings certificates and savings stamps. The loyalty of Letchworth citizens was evident when the target of £100,000 was surpassed with a final amount of £189,511 being saved. The Letchworth Savings Committee carried on for some years after the war.

A Messerschmitt 109, which had been shot down, was on display in Letchworth. It stood in front of the Council Offices on the Arena car park.

I recall we had a Wings for Victory savings campaign and Letchworth decided to raise enough by street collections to purchase a Spitfire. The target was £5000. This doesn't seem much by today's costs - but then it was a great amount. The Spitfire was bought in March 1940.

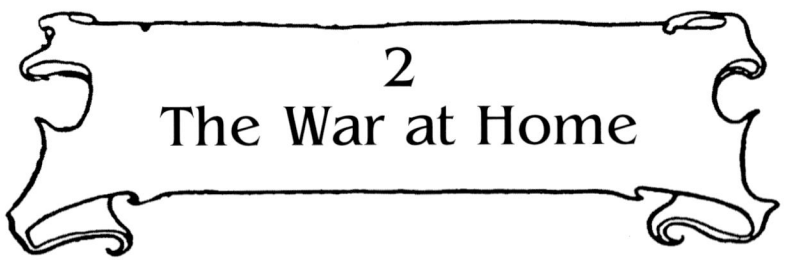

2
The War at Home

Hardship and Rationing

The war, of course, brought much hardship, with rationing and shortages. Gardens were used to grow vegetables or even keep chickens and people learnt to "make do and mend", but there were also treats to be had from time to time. Schools also played their part in the war effort.

From the School we did our bit for the war effort by going potato picking, and I can well remember 50 very clean children going in a coach to a local farm to pick potatoes all day and 50 very muddy children arriving back in the coach much to the horror of the driver. I think for the two days potato picking we were rewarded with a magnificent sum of nine shillings and six pence.

We also, instead of our school games, were encouraged to pick dandelions off the school playing field which my father didn't think very much about. For the first holiday in the summer - our school holiday - it was decided that it was not good to have children about for six weeks not supervised so we had two weeks at home and then we had four weeks at school with various activities. Needless to say, this only happened once.

I didn't notice the war making us hard up for things at school, but of course we did not know what a banana looked like, nor an orange. I remember it must have been well through the war they did start to have ice-creams up Leys Avenue, at one of the shops there. They used to have them once a fortnight and we used to queue up. I used to go and queue up and try to get one for my Mum as well. I would queue up with my school cap on, then put it in my pocket and go back and have another go.

We had a lovely long garden with rustic rose arches, a lawn and a long vegetable garden, which we used to help our mother with and pick the fruit and vegetables. Most houses in Letchworth had these long gardens, a godsend during the war years, as we were expected to 'Dig for Victory', the famous slogan of the time.

Food was rationed and took on a great importance at the time. I remember one day at Westbury School, thinking of the scarcity of food, I took some little fairy cakes to school for my lunch. Mother had made them in little pleated paper cases. A little boy next to me called Dennis, asked for my paper cases full of crumbs and ate them, paper and all! I was later to find out that he came from the orphanage, Briar Patch, on the outskirts of the town. He must have been hungry to have eaten the paper. I told my mother when I got home and she was very moved, so much so, that even though there was rationing, there was an extra lunch for Dennis from then on. We would visit him in the orphanage on Saturday afternoons. Then when he was transferred to the Grange at Stevenage we continued to visit for some time. Gradually it tailed off and we lost track of him.

People with gardens, however small, were urged to turn the gardens over to growing food so a 'Dig for Victory' campaign started and most evenings householders would be busy digging out the flowers and planting potatoes and cabbages instead. Every morning on the radio, the Minister for Food would give a recipe for some weird and wonderful dish. The idea was to inform the public about the kind of food that was nutritious and available.

The radio talk that really intrigued me was about haybox cooking. The idea was to line a strong wooden box with several layers of newspaper or brown paper then cover the paper with an old blanket. This was then packed firmly with clean dry hay, leaving a few nests to hold jam jars. The food would then be prepared in the usual way, brought to the boil and cooked for up to thirty minutes. Then the cooking pan would be removed from the stove, wrapped in a piece of flannel and put in the haybox. The jam jars would be filled with a pudding or two, and the whole box would then be covered with a cushion, the lid fastened down and the food would continue cooking for several hours in the box. We were advised to cook rabbits, which could add variety to our diets, but were given no advice as to where to find the rabbits, so made do with the few that found their way into the shops, if we were lucky.

My Mum would take us out first thing in the morning pea picking to earn enough money to get a bit of breakfast for us. We went to Rutts Farm, opposite the Letchworth Cemetery. He had pea fields in there - and brussel fields and potatoes. He was a dairy farmer as well but there were the fields attached there. Sometimes we went right out of the town - but we all went on the back of a lorry or a tractor and trailer. We had some bread and marge if you were lucky and Mum had a bottle of tea and a bottle of water and that was your lot. We were happy and if somebody was lucky enough to have a fish paste sandwich, you wanted one. "Coo, how come that they've got fish paste and we've got bread and marge?" Bit of bread and dripping if you were lucky.

I remember my dad keeping chickens because, of course, eggs were in short supply and quite a few people around our way kept chickens too. I can remember on two occasions going with my father a long distance - once over to Fowlmere and another time over Stevenage to get these chickens so we could have a supply of eggs.

It was a hard time for my mother, and I can remember her helping a lady in Bedford Road with her cleaning, a Mrs Reece. I expect it was bringing in some much needed extra money. My sister was at Westbury School, so I had to sit on a stool in the kitchen whilst my mother was working there, and then at the table in the parlour as she moved around the house. As I was only a toddler, Mrs Reece would give me a tin of pretty coloured beads to play with.

There Were Oranges in Letchworth

But No Queues

LETCHWORTH'S allocation of oranges was on sale on Monday, but there were no queues, as on previous occasions, because it had been decided that all shops should sell on the

I don't know how my mum did it. She somehow put on Christmas for us. She used to keep chickens and she used to fatten up a couple of cockerels. She also used to keep rabbits for meat. We weren't allowed to pet them at all. Mum always fattened up half a dozen cockerels for the table for Christmas. She would sell some and she would sell rabbit meat. In return somebody else would have chickens laying eggs so she would pass eggs on to Mum.

I was fortunate because I was allowed perhaps two ounces more of butter, and certain different bits, because of my illness, you see. But you know, everything worked out well really.

There were many hardships. I still save string, and even now I am careful with paper, because you could not get any paper to reckon up on. We had £100 and £50 envelopes to put notes in, and when we had used one we always saved the paper to write on, and it became second nature. If you had a piece of paper you saved it. The few years we had to make these savings seemed to have stayed for us.

Everything seemed to be in short supply, a great treat was the odd parcel from America with raisins and Spam! When my sister married in 1947 'dockets' ' were needed for bed linen and we all saved our clothing coupons for a special dress (seven each).

During a very damp October and November we would get up early in the misty morning, whilst the cows were being milked, to gather mushrooms in the field near Bedford Road. They were to supplement our rations, which they certainly did, as they were huge. One was so big we had to cut it to get it into the frying pan. The farmer's fields where we gathered them are now covered in houses, from Bedford Road to over Beech Hill and all around the area up to the Pix Brook and opposite Standalone Farm entrance. That area used to be all open meadows right up to the backs of the houses in Wilbury Road.

We used to get so excited when the occasional parcel arrived from India, because of rationing. My father would send lots of sweets, fudges and chocolate. The parcels would all be sewn up in hessian, to make sure they arrived safely and intact from their long journey. Sometimes they contained presents, handmade Indian tooled leather bags and purses. One present was a handmade silver bracelet hung with silver sixpences, all of my birth year, 1938. I was very proud of this and it was put in the box of treasures with grandmother's postcard. He used to draw little pictures to amuse us and I started drawing pictures on my letters until it became a regular thing. I used to listen to the radio as I drew. I remember some wonderful programmes like Children's Hour with Uncle Mac, Larry the Lamb, Donald Peers and 'By a Babbling Brook', Dick Barton, Arthur Askey (Busy Bee) and many more. These are mixed with memories of huddling round a small fire to keep warm, having heavy colds, mother dishing out our ration of cod liver oil, orange juice and stuffing Thermogene under my liberty bodice. Thermogene was a bright orangey-red cotton wool substance meant to keep our chest warm, either to prevent colds or keep us warm, when we had one.

I remember the cafe. I know I didn't dream it. It was a treat - it was dead facing the Palace Cinema - it was only there during the War years. It was a little white hut of some kind, because I was only a little kid remember. On rare occasions when Mum took us all to the pictures one of the treats would be to come out and go across the road and you would get a cheese roll or a cheese cracker. Mum would have a cup of tea and we would have to share a cup. Then on the days she was quite well off, which wasn't very often, we would go to Whitehead's Garage and we would come home in style - we would come home in a taxi and I felt like a queen. It was fantastic.

Rationing was introduced and as we sold food which was on coupons, life at the end of the month became a matter of having to count all the coupons and send them to the local Food Office. Cigarettes became short but we did try - or my father did - to look after his regulars to see that they all got the brand that they smoked.

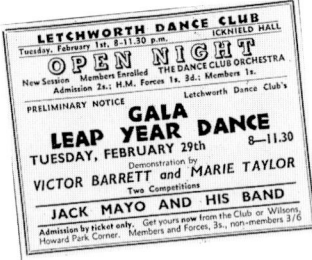

I used to queue up after school very often to get the rations. We had our ration books at the Co-op in Eastcheap and then take those home one day a week. My Mother would get what she could and I had always got a two shilling piece in my satchel, if I went into the town. I always had to report home first and go to the town afterwards. I would look at Mr. Broughton's - the Pork Butchers - and various places to see if there was a queue and to see if he had sausages off ration or liver off ration or something like that. My school friends and I queued up outside the Health Food Stores for cakes. Sometimes you could get little cakes. If you saw a queue you joined it. The sausages were horrible, they were mostly bread. Things were very short and I admired the housewives so very much because I never went home without having some sort of meal - a hot meal - on the table and I think that our mothers were absolutely wonderful - our fathers too, for all that they did.

I recall taking the family ration books to John Wells grocery shop in Leys Avenue and Dewhurst the butcher in Station Road. Apparently we were all much healthier then on what would now seem like microscopic rations! We got good bread from Notts and Wegmullers, we eked out the butter ration with cashew or peanut butter from the Health Food Stores or Radnage Agency. My parents kept fierce, well fed Rhode Island Reds, we had a plum and apple tree, soft fruit bushes, and grew peas, beans and tomatoes. Any other green grocery we needed we bought at Cheethams, presided, over by Margaret at her school desk as the money till, and by Mr. Cheetham in his apron and straw hat. Fenners and Beddoes for papers, sweets, and tobacco and definitely Hoopers the chemist with its lovely coloured glass containers in the window. I get quite sentimental when remembering Moss's, the Co-operative, Spinks, Nicholls and Tilleys the drapers with the fascinating wired system for containers which sent your change between floors. I loved Brookers the ironmonger with the drawers and rows of nails, washers and tools presided over by assistants who knew just what you wanted and where everything was.

Rationing was still on when I got married in 1953 and I remember I cried at the end of the fortnight after I got home from my honeymoon because I had used all my rations up and I had another two days to go. I was really in tears. One of my older neighbours asked me if I had got some cheese. I had the tiniest bit of cheese and so she taught me how to make cheese, potato and herb pie so I got through. I really thought we were going to starve. There were no cookery lessons at school during the War and my mother would not let me touch her rations - her precious rations - so when I got married I can tell you I was not much of a cook. But still we managed and shortly - about 1955 - everything came off.

I remember the end of rationing, especially the end of sweet rationing. There was a shop on the corner of Bedford Road called Ottaways. I remember standing in a queue there and getting sweets for the first time.

Rationing was a problem, of course. It's funny how many mothers gave up eating eggs and used their ration to put in a cake - that sort of thing - because by the end of the War the rations were very small by today's standards. On the other hand we were adequately and properly fed - it was a very well thought out scheme. Children, babies and expectant mothers were very well catered for so that they were healthy.

You could not take it for granted that you were going to have a pair of shoes or a new dress - that was out of the question. Food was scarce. I don't know how my mum managed - I really don't know how she managed - she must have been a magician. She taught me plenty that kept me in good stead - I mean I have had 13 children. Her thrifty way of life because of the rationing has always helped me. We cook up for a month - we have plenty there to stock us out and when the grand-children come round I can give them bits and pieces as well - they're happy.

We had the ration book. I remember going to Beddoes in Station Road. He would open when he felt like it. Old Percy Beddoe was quite a character really. I can remember coming out of Hillshott School and Brolio the ice cream man would be there with his horse. He used to come up from Hitchin. It was very nice ice cream. I can remember the "Stop Me and Buy One" (Walls) coming round with his tricycle. That was before the War. I had one mystery I could never understand. I could go into Woolworth's (they had like a snack bar in there during the War) and they had banana sandwiches. I could never understand where they got the bananas from. We could only get dried bananas. I found out afterwards they were either parsnips or turnips mashed up with banana flavouring, but they were quite nice, so I quite enjoyed them. So that answered it.

It was amazing how quickly rumours travelled round the town when food that was unrationed, or other supplies arrived. The queues would form in minutes and I spent many hours waiting for those precious strawberries or perhaps hair grips, combs, or anything! Hair grips were a necessity in those days as many women did their hair in bangs that had to be clipped into place.

Clothes could only be obtained with coupons, and getting dressed up for an evening out, especially for ladies, required ingenuity. Some people were lucky to have relations and friends in the United States who sent parcels to them.

Shoes were very difficult to get hold of and most shoes in the shops were of the utility variety. When word got round that a new consignment of shoes had come into a shop in Letchworth or Hitchin, we would spend an entire lunch hour queuing outside the shoe shop in the hope of getting a decent pair of shoes before returning to work, in the knowledge that all the shoes would be sold by the following day and there would not be another consignment for months. My sister and I were lucky in that we received clothes, dress material and shoes from our American cousins during the war. They once sent a large fruit cake and a box of popcorn, which none of us had ever seen or heard of. Neither Mrs Clements nor ourselves knew what to do with it, so she decided to put it in a saucepan which was pre-heated. As soon as the popcorn hit the pan, it started bouncing up to the kitchen ceiling, while the children laughed and jumped up and down. Finally we gave the popcorn to a lady at the end of the street who kept chickens, so it wasn't wasted.

Shoe leather and mending shoes was a problem as rationing made things difficult. I remember one of my uncles would help mother out by mending them, when we could get the materials. Otherwise we used to cut pieces of cardboard to put inside the shoes when they got thin, and even block the hole with a piece of chewing gum, that Pamela, my elder cousin, could always provide. Mostly we wore little metal studs or tacks on the bottom of the heels and toes of our shoes, to counteract the wear and need of mending. These packets of studs hung in Mrs Waller's corner shop, on the right hand side of the door.

To be correctly dressed for a day or night on the town, stockings, even in summer, were an essential part of a girl's outfit, but when stockings were unavailable we painted our legs with a cream the colour of ochre, obtainable at the chemists. To add to the authenticity, a friend would pencil in a dark line on each back leg, to represent the join in real stockings, but I'm sure no one was fooled. If out on the town, a hat was also worn to complete the ensemble. On reflection, we must have looked comical in our best summer outfits, smart hats and yellow legs! Nylon stockings came on the scene in the late 1940's, Kayser Bondor of Baldock being one of the earlier manufacturers in the region, so the yellow leg cream became finally and thankfully redundant.

As a teenager in the fifties, unless you were well off financially and able to buy extra coupons on the black market, clothes were always a problem, and the choices of colour drab (to make them last). But when the sixties arrived, it all changed, and high fashion came into its own again. There was a marvellous little Boutique in Eastcheap, whose name I forget; but though the quality of the clothes was excellent, even an ordinary working girl could save up to look smart and feminine. To buy the same quality today would go into three figures instead of the five or six guineas we paid.

Rationing was tight and clothes were only available with the necessary clothing coupons, so keeping up to date with current fashions was not easy, but dear Rhoda could recycle old garments and bring them up to date with her sewing machine which she allowed us to use. I remember during a summer heatwave, I longed for a dip in the swimming pool, but without a swimming costume, it was out of the question. Arriving home from work, Rhoda presented me with a two-piece swimsuit. She had cut down her husband's one-piece costume to make me a very up to date swimsuit. The shortage of clothing coupons inspired women to make new clothes from old, and very smart they were too.

Keeping warm was a challenge during the War.

One of the greatest comforts in the homes of today must undoubtably be central healing where all rooms can be comfortably heated in winter. During the war and post war years, the only form of heating in most homes was a coal fire in the living room, around which the family gathered on cold winter nights to listen to the wireless or to follow whatever hobbies they enjoyed. As a result, our fronts were toasted whilst our backs were chilled from icy draughts blowing through ill fitting doors and windows. The compulsory blackout curtains kept some draughts at bay, as well as concealing the lighted windows from the crews in any overhead enemy aircraft. Bedrooms were seldom heated, even though there was an open fireplace in at least one bedroom in every house. Fuel for fires was in short supply; and a bedroom fire would only be lit if there was a confinement, or if a child was ill.

Another commodity in short supply was rubber, so replacing old rubber hot water bottles was impossible. At best a hot water bottle warmed a very small part of the bed, so we would use heated bricks wrapped in flannel to bring a little extra warmth to our beds on cold winter nights. I'm not sure when electric blankets came on the scene, but I do not recollect any during the war years. Metal hot water bottles, together with aluminium pots and pans were collected for melting down and re-using for the war effort. We had to make do with what we could salvage from our kitchen utensils, as all the best pots and pans were taken away and utilised in a different form by the military.

Public transport

Despite the hardship and problems, some things were not so bad, including public transport. Since petrol was rationed this was the only way to get around.

One item that was the tops in wartime was undoubtedly public transport. People from surrounding towns and villages were working in Letchworth and they were bussed into the factories from about seven am and all bussed home again in the evenings. It was possible to stand at a bus stop and have up to three buses going in the same direction. They would also be lined up in Works Road in the evening to take the workers home again. The trains from London to Hitchin kept up a regular service right through till eleven pm, so an evening out in Hitchin was possible as you could be sure of a train home before midnight. Of course there were very few private cars or taxis on the roads then. The main hazard was walking home from the station in the blackout. We all carried torches as there were no streetlights, but the torches, which had to be trained on the ground, giving only a small pool of light, were useless on a very dark or foggy night. Most Saturdays we would get the train to London and enjoy a visit to England's capital city, the return fare costing one shilling and nine pence.

Holidays at Home

People were encouraged to "holiday at home" during the war and leisure activities were curtailed. The people of Letchworth, and especially the children, had no problem making their own entertainment. The Churches also provided places to spend time.

During the long school holidays we used a wind-up gramophone and an old record to make up our own sing-songs, dances and concerts in our back garden. We seemed to invite all the children from the neighbourhood to our garden for these!

During the war time there was a parson came down from London and he took over the canteen at Pioneer Laundry in Pixmore Avenue. He used to give little sermons there, and he attracted all us children. We used to go from school there. He took over the laundry canteen on Sunday and used to encourage us to go and listen to him giving these sermons. I used to go to St Paul's and later to the Central Methodist. I think I was attracted there because they used to have a

Holidays at home

This year thousands of London's workers will be spending their well-earned holidays at home. London and its countryside retain many of their attractions even in this fifth year of war, and London Transport will do its best to meet local travel requirements. But transport resources are severely limited and the services are primarily designed to meet the essential needs of those not on holiday. The services cannot be strengthened.

Londoners on holiday should think twice therefore before making even the short 1½d. journey and, if travel is necessary, they should avoid the rush hours. In this way, they will earn the gratitude of their fellow-workers and of London Transport.

Think twice before you travel

Guild on a Tuesday night where we used to be able to play table tennis and have beetle drives and things like that.

We went to several different Sunday Schools, St Thomas's, Elim Churchs' Sunshine Corner and the Free Church. We used to win prizes of books with lovely ornate bookplates in the front. We received picture stamps of the religious calendar on every visit, to fill a collecting book, so if you missed a Sunday you had a stamp missing. The churches of Letchworth had lots of things happening during those years. I remember sing-song evening and activities. It was a time of blackout curtains and no streetlights, in the hope that this would deter bombs being dropped, so these activities were much appreciated.

Towns had to organise holiday events and people were encouraged to "holiday at home'. Several events were organised in Letchworth. There were always events at the 'ozone' swimming pool on the Common. Gala swimming events were a great attraction and I remember one year - probably 1942 - when Eric Portman the film star came to Letchworth to judge a bathing beauty contest. The entrants were some of the lovely Letchworth lassies - all with superb figures I recall.

Holidays at home was the theme for war-time holidays. Travel was severely restricted. Train timetables unreliable. Petrol was rationed and coupons only available for essential purposes. There was a basic petrol allowance for every vehicle, which was taxed. This was very limited and many people laid up their cars for the duration.

During the war, as part of the "Holidays at Home" scheme promoted by the Council, my father organised a series of weekend concerts given there by such well known brass or military bands as that of the Welsh Guards. They also brought with them such well-known singers as Isobel Bailie and Nancy Evans. My mother had been a singer when young and I still remember the thrill we both felt, when we entertained Nancy Evans in our house overnight and listened to her rehearsing with our piano!

War time housing

A number of people moved into Letchworth during the war from other parts of the country. Housing had to be found for them, and sometimes life was a little different from that which they were used to.

Jackmans Place was where I grew up. All the gardens had hedgerows there, and people had chickens, so you woke up in the mornings with the cockerel. It was quite common then.

During the war years many country people were drafted into the busy industrial areas such as Letchworth, and made their homes in industrial towns and cities for the duration of the war. People were allowed to opt for the forces, the land girls or war work in the factories. Some girls working at Lloyds came from the north of England and also from Wales, and you would have to give a very good reason for refusing to work in a munitions factory miles away from your home town. Of course all those workers had to find accommodation and this is where the billeting officer came in. He or she would have a list of homes with rooms to spare and even though householders did not wish to take in war workers as paying guests, they would need to put a very strong argument against accepting them.

My sister and I stayed at the home of Mrs Clements in Hillshott. Mrs Clements was a kind and gentle lady, who made me feel so much at home that soon all homesickness for my Irish farm disappeared. I arrived in Letchworth on a Saturday and the following morning my sister took me on a tour of the Garden City. There were flowers everywhere, with lots of daffodils growing in the nearby Howard Gardens, I picked a bunch of daffodils and gave them to Mrs Clements as a thank you for her kindness. When I told her where I had obtained the flowers she was quite upset and did not want to accept them. She then explained that picking the flowers that were growing in the parks was not allowed. At home on our farm, daffodils grew everywhere in the spring. They grew in fields and hedgerows and by the side of roads. We could fill every available container in the house with those lovely first flowers of the year. My first lesson in England was "when in Rome do as the Romans do, and when in the first Garden City of Letchworth, don't pick the flowers"!

Amongst these newcomers to the town were Indians who came to train at the Ascot Training Centre. In 1941 the King and Queen visited the training Centre - an event which caused quite a stir in the town.

In 1941 the Ascot Government Training Centre played an important role in training Indian technicians in engineering skills so that they could return to play their part in India's War effort. They were housed in various places, but the People's House offered the main accommodation. The Indians became a familiar sight in Letchworth with many Sikhs wearing turbans, something new for Letchworth in those days.

Many years after the War, when travelling abroad on business for my own company, I met an Indian who, when he learned that I came from Letchworth, told me he was a trainee at the Centre when the King and Queen visited. He said he had fond memories of the Garden City - "The people were so kind and made us welcome". He also told me that the training did him in good stead because he was currently a director of a large Indian engineering firm employing over 1000 people.

The King visits Letchworth

I can remember vividly the King and Queen visiting Letchworth in September/October 1941. This was supposed to be a closely-guarded secret and nobody was supposed to know anything about it but, as usual, the news leaked out, and crowds started to gather at the top of Station Road. My father - who was a Special Constable - was called out about half an hour before the King and Queen arrived to control the crowds. His years in office as a Special Constable had a sort of 'Dad's Army' aura about it, especially the time he was called to guard the Police Station and given a gun with no ammunition - that was locked in a desk. If he wanted to fire he was supposed to go in and ask the Police Sergeant for it.

The King and Queen visited Letchworth in October 1941 to visit the Indians and were conducted on a tour of the Training Centre. They visited the Peoples House in Station Road and a huge crowd gathered and cheered them on their way. I was the Press Association representative on the occasion of their visit (as well as Citizen reporter). The press and others were entertained to lunch at the then Garden City Hotel at the bottom of Station Road. I recall I had my leg pulled - I was thanked 'officially' for the courtesy of the Press Association in providing the beer for the occasion. The reason for the misunderstanding was because the beer was capped with bold letters PA - really meaning Pale Ale of course.

King George VI and Queen Elizabeth visit Letchworth in 1941.

King George VI and Queen Elizabeth visit the Ascot Government Training Centre in 1941.

Other memories regarding the war years, was the visit of the King and Queen Elizabeth, on Thursday 25th September 1941. I was then a pupil at Letchworth Grammar School. The Headmaster, Mr Wilkinson, came round one afternoon to confirm the rumour that we already had and that was sweeping the town, that our King and Queen were coming to visit the town. The school, facing across the Town Square, as it was called then, he said, "You had better go out and stand on the path and see them as they come". My father worked, in what is now the Town Hall, the Council Offices as it was known, so I went to his office and had a grandstand view as the car came round in front of the Museum, into Eastcheap, down the road to a building in Station Road that is now the Four Emblems Club. Later on we went down there to see them go from there down Station Road on their way to the Government Training Hostel, known to the residents of the town as the Ascot, where they met up with the people who were there learning trades - learning skills to do with industry to do with war work. Later, we understand they left at about six o'clock in the evening.

Being a reporter on the spot I carried my own Pathe Cine camera - the cheapest version of a 9.5mm camera - and had a good opportunity for close-ups of the King and Queen.

Ernest Bevin the then Minister of Labour in the Wartime Cabinet also visited the Ascot Training Centre with the Royal party.

I remember going to the Training Centre when the Queen Mother, as she is now, came with her husband. I was about seven or eight, at Hillshott, and we all came up and lined the road here.

There was a film taken of this event, which was shown on the news at the cinema.

King George VI and Queen Elizabeth on their visit to Letchworth 1941.

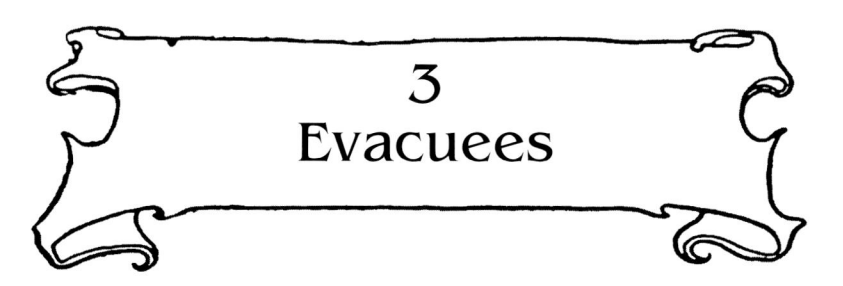

3
Evacuees

Evacuees arrived in Letchworth at the start of the War. Many residents remember them arriving. Quite a few stayed in the town after the War ended, and they too remember the day they arrived.

On 1 September 1939, two days before the war started, the town filled up with evacuees. I think every house in the town that possibly could, had one or two children, some children anyway. So of course every mother, every householder, had billeting forms, because they had so much a week each to keep the children. I can't remember how much it was now.

The Billeting Office

I was in the Billeting Office so that is a different view so far as the evacuation. At that time the town became extremely full with all these various evacuees - some had gone back - but even so there were an awful lot here and so it became a closed area. That meant that anyone who wanted to have visitors for any length of time had to fill in a form and so we were the ones who had to deal with that. It meant quite a lot of work too. I remember one couple who wanted to adopt a little boy. They had to apply for the child to come into the town. I had an uncle and aunt who lived in the Chatham area, which was being bombed at the time. My uncle was ill and so my aunt, who had come to live with us, had to apply for him to come in.

At that time we had two Billeting Officers and a woman joined us as well. Her husband was in the Army - so she was on her own, but it was a very worrying time because she was worried about her husband in the Army and the other two ladies were worried about their husbands still in London. Earlier on during the Blitz one of the husbands was in the Fire Service. Naturally they were extremely worried about what was going on because he was on duty and from Letchworth we could see the red glow in the sky from the fires.

At the outbreak of War I was still travelling backwards and forwards to Cambridge school. I was at Secretarial College there, but when it was realised we would be travelling by train the Headmistress, who was rather an old-fashioned lady, was very worried about us getting into trouble or something, and so our course was postponed or, in fact, it really came to an end.

I then had to find myself a job and I ended up at the Billeting Office. At that time, this was in one of the rooms downstairs in the Library and it was rather chaotic because nobody had any experience at all of dealing with all these thousands of people that had descended on Letchworth. However, there were masses of volunteers all pulling together and they managed really quite well. When we had got sorted out a bit more we moved upstairs into the Library Lecture Room because there was very much more room in there and we had to have a store for bedding things as well. The staff consisted of a Billeting Officer and Clerks and they were dealing with the receipts from the Post Office because if you had an evacuee you had an allowance which you obtained from the Post Office and the receipts came back to our Billeting Office. Then they were entered up on a card index. Each household had a card and there were various details of whom and what evacuees they had, if they needed any bedding that was entered up. That was my job. I had no experience whatsoever in dealing with things but it's surprising what you can do when you try.

So there was I, a 16-year-old, sorting out bedding, mattresses and enamel bowls and all sorts of things for people who had not got enough and getting the dockets for all that organised. Some of them just had not got room for evacuees really and we had to re-organise their houses and their bedding problems and all that sort of thing. That was another sideline that I had and then when the evacuees left the house all bedding had to be returned and fumigated. The old ambulance from the fever hospital, the isolation hospital which is now Rosehill, was used for taking them for fumigation. When they came back to our office the smell from the fumes was absolutely horrible but we learned to live with that.

Another lot of people who arrived were the women working in the factories. They were known as War Workers. We had various people there - with all sorts of problems. One party came from the Orkneys and some of them had never been on the mainland before so it was quite different for them.

The children that came were not always terribly clean - to say the least - so they had to be sorted out at the Minor Ailments Clinic which was at Letchworth House where Sister Freeman was in charge. That's now the Ambassador Hotel but at that time it had been a private house owned by the Ewart family of Ewart Geysers but they had left Letchworth during the War so the house was used for this Clinic.

Some of the mothers and children who came out were very short of money and so they had to apply to the Relieving Officer - a Mr. James - who came up from Baldock several times a week to see to it. He had to consult with the Billeting Officer and we had to sort out their problems too.

Receiving Evacuees

Before the outbreak of War each household was visited and asked to take evacuees if and when War was declared. The numbers were according to the number of rooms in your house. So if you were a family of three as we were - mother, father and one daughter - we lived in a five roomed house and so we would have to take two evacuees. So as I was a girl my mother thought it would be a good idea if we took two girls and she would prefer younger ones if possible - we were given that sort of choice. The larger houses were allocated for mothers and children.

On the 1st September the evacuees started to arrive and it went on through that weekend and, of course, War was declared on the Sunday. Whole schools came from Stoke Newington and from Tottenham and there were so many children that they had to be taken round in "Green's" furniture vans. It seemed rather unfeeling at the time but we had to get them round somehow.

We had expected two little cockney children -

THE CITIZEN, SEPTEMBER 8th, 1939

HOW THE EVACUEES ARRIVED IN LETCHWORTH

The Scenes at the Railway Station

as they were coming from London - but we didn't get them at all - we got two teenage girls who were Jewish. Inga was a German and she had recently arrived from Berlin. She had been rescued by the Quakers and sent to an uncle in London who immediately registered her at the local school so that she was evacuated straight away. The other girl was Doris and she was from a Polish family, although she had been born in London. It was rather difficult as they had to share a bedroom and even a bed and at that time Poland was being invaded by the Germans but at least they had the fact that they were Jewish in common.

I can tell you one rather strange thing that happened with Doris. After she had got settled in, her parents used to come down regularly to see her and they belonged to the family who produced a very well-known make of skirt. One weekend her brother came down on his own - he cycled actually because he was young and fit and able to do things like that - I suppose he must have been about 18 at the time. Anyway, he spent some time with us and the next weekend the mother arrived with a skirt for me. My parents said "Well how on earth did you know the right size?" So they said "Well, our Maxi looked her over". Of course, this tickled my Father tremendously and there was a sort of saying in our house after that - "Our Maxi looked her over". So that was Doris.

Now Inga was very lucky because she met up with a couple of children that she had been to school with in Berlin and they were billeted just below us in Lytton Avenue so they were able to meet up quite often. In fact they arranged that they would have their Friday night Jewish little service in our back bedroom. This involved the lighting of candles. Well my mother didn't mind this business of having their service in there - or get-together - whatever it was - but she did rather object to the candles being left burning all night. So they said "Oh well its a sin if you blow them out" so I think she said that she would prefer to have the sin and not burnt curtains. So that was those two children.

Of course it was very difficult for the people coming from London to settle in Letchworth because life was so different here and I think we did have one fish and chip shop but there were certainly no pubs. Also their way of life was so different from ours - there was no television so we didn't really know much about them. I don't suppose some of the London children had ever been out in the country before. Anyway there were all sorts of problems, as you can imagine, and everybody descended on our office and got into quite a state sometimes. You had to be very tactful.

But there were success stories and I remember a childless couple who adopted a Jewish girl and she became one of their family. Then, we had foreign refugees coming, of course, from various countries that had been invaded and also we had Servicemen looking for their wives who had disappeared from home in London. Also in our office

Bexhill evacuees in front of an air raid shelter.

we had two helpers who had come out with their children from Stoke Newington and Tottenham and they were actually acting as Liaison Officers dealing with the mass of complaints that we received. In that way we managed to sort things out pretty well I think.

After a while there was a threat of invasion on the south coast so that meant that the schools from that area were evacuated. We had schools from Bexhill. St. Marks School - which I think came from the village of Cooden - near Bexhill - was billeted on Willian so they settled down quite happily there. Then there was Downe School - I think those children went to Pixmore and maybe some of the other schools − I'm not too sure - and then the Bexhill County School was sent to the Grammar School. Now these children seemed to settle better than the Londoners, so a few of them - in fact quite a few of them - stayed on in Letchworth after the War ended and settled here permanently. Our two Jewish girls had departed - they didn't settle terribly well - so we then took in two little children from the Downe School and we got on very well with them and they stayed with us for quite a while until the emergency finished on the South Coast. Then their mother came and took them away.

The next lot to arrive was the Bloomsbury Technical School and they also came to the Grammar School and then we took in Rhona who was studying photography. That was really quite interesting to have somebody doing something interesting like that because at that time there wasn't the interest in photography as there is nowadays.

Of course we had evacuees billeted on us. A technical school from London, Camberwell I think, shared teaching facilities with the Grammar School, and its head teacher, Miss Cummings, stayed with us until the bombing ceased and they returned to London. Then for some time we gave a home to two secondary school girls, sisters, from Bodiam, Sussex. One of them was very homesick and sharing a bedroom with her I remember she sometimes cried herself to sleep. She was old enough to realise the danger of invasion faced by the South Coast towns and was worried about her parents.

When the War started my wife was working as nurse in a London hospital and her mother was alone in her house at Eastholm Green except for an invalid old lady that she looked after. The authorities billeted two young ladies on her. The house had one large bedroom and two small ones, so the two young women shared the large one. When my wife returned to Letchworth to have her baby in 1942, she had one of the small bedrooms and her mother had the other. During the war each of the billettees married a serviceman and when they and I returned we had three families, two old ladies and a child, all occupying the same small house. The council sorted it out as soon as they could, but it took some time. It was a good example of what housing shortage meant in 1946.

On the 3rd September a lot of evacuees from London came to Letchworth and I remember my parents taking dining chairs out into the street. The evacuees sat along the street until people went out and chose them to come into their houses. Our evacuees were a woman and her son from Walthamstow but they went back after a few weeks as there was no bombing yet. After that the town was given over to War work and it was compulsory that you had War Workers in the house. We had an American girl called Olivia Jaquest who, although America was not yet in the War, along with quite a lot of other Americans came to help the War effort. She lived with us and worked at the K & L Steel Founders and then she was posted somewhere else later on. We had a Czechoslovakian Jewish girl who had left Czechoslovakia on her own as the Germans walked in. Her father had got tickets for her and her sister. Her sister stayed with the parents and after the War none of her family were ever heard of again. Her name was Marian Leitner and she stayed with us until the end of the War and she worked at the Marmet.

When the evacuees came to Letchworth, I wasn't really compelled to have them because I didn't enjoy very good health. But I saw these two little girls standing out the front, which nobody had taken so I went out, and I said "Oh I'll have them". They came in and I can remember my husband used to give them a few coppers, because they helped me to wipe up. After they went I had another two.

I had a family from London, relations to my neighbours in Eldefield. They were the mother and two daughters, but the mother was stone deaf and I had to get right near her and shout in her ear to make her listen. I got in such a habit that I was doing it to my husband. He used to say "Well I'm not Liza, you know".

I remember clearly the day that these evacuees came by train into Letchworth station as I was a Girl Guide and had to be part of the escort party taking these unfortunate children and pregnant and nursing mothers to their host accommodations. They were first taken to the Broadway cinema and then, column by column, were allocated around the town. Some of us had to clean and sweep the seats and aisles of the cinema when it was emptied of the sad occupancy. We had, firstly, a girl from London and later a girl from Bexhill, who my sister and me teased remorselessly. Our parents turned the sitting room into a bedroom for us as they considered that it was safer in the event of a bomb dropping.

Another person I befriended was a little German girl called Ursula. She was staying with a family in Hallmead. Because of the War people were not too friendly at first, but I got on well with her, and we spent a lot of time together. I have lots of photos of her, but did not keep up the writing when she eventually returned to Munster in Westphalia and have now lost track.

Evacuees at school

The children who came to Letchworth had to attend the local schools, which caused very large classes but also gave the children of Letchworth the chance to make friends with the new arrivals.

We had an evacuee living with us when we lived in Green Lane. She did not come to Norton School - she went to the village. There were a lot of the evacuees went down to St. Nicholas School. Gracie Fields' Orphanage was evacuated to Wilbury Turrets at the top of Wilbury Road. Some of them I presume came to Norton School - they were rather distinctive as they had a very smart uniform. They were Junior School children. I don't know how long they were there or what happened to them afterwards. I remember they used to wear grey gymslips, which was different to us as we wore navy blue. There were other evacuees there but a lot of the children who were evacuated to the Norton area seemed to go down to the village school, because, of course, we were absolutely packed at Norton School. We had 50 children to a class at one time during those years. I mean we always had about 45 - 48 but I remember my father getting one report saying number in class was, I think, 53. The school was very crowded. We shared the Grammar School with pupils from Bexhill County School who were evacuated to Letchworth. It was extremely overcrowded for a time - Letchworth pupils had to remain on the ground floor.

I was at the Grammar School 1941 to 1944 during the war. We had evacuees in Jackmans Place. There was Russell, a lad from London, who lived in the cul de sac in Jackmans Place. I was friendly with him; and Cyril was in Jackmans Place just where the recreation ground entrance is. Mrs Males and Ron came to Mrs Mynott's. I was friendly with Ken, her son. I don't think many evacuees came to the Grammar School, that I knew. Presumably they went to the secondary school, Pixmore. I remember Ivor. He came and appeared in Campers Road. I went on my first cycling holiday with him when I was 16, and we cycled round to Felixstowe and places.

1939 coincided with my having to leave school at the ripe old age of 14 years. My last memories of Norton Road School being the necessity of having to share with the "Vaccies" from London.

We were assessed for evacuees and a Jewish family came from London with a young son to live with us. School was shared - sometimes we spent half of each day on outdoor pursuits so that the city children could use our classroom.

Being an evacuee

I first heard the name of Letchworth in 1940 when we learned that it was to this town that our school - East Sussex County School for Girls - was to be evacuated. My parents made enquiries at the local reference library and discovered that our destination was somewhere rather special though I don't think I knew then just what was its claim to fame.

Up until then our south coast town, Bexhill-on-Sea, had been considered a safe area - we had, in fact, received evacuees from London and had been sharing our school buildings with another grammar school. After Dunkirk, however, invasion seemed imminent; the London school departed for Wales and preparations were made to evacuate local schoolchildren. I suppose because we were to go as a school, I think we were more excited by the novelty than apprehensive about the future. I don't remember much about the journey - except that it was a long hot day in the train, which was somehow routed round London with no need to change trains.

My first experience of Letchworth was walking up the Broadway from the station to the Grammar School, where we were greeted with very welcome glasses of lemonade - our first taste of Letchworth hospitality. After that we were put into coaches and driven round the town to be "distributed" to various homes and introduced to our hostesses, who had little choice but to accept us. I think at that time, and certainly later, the authorities counted up the number of bedrooms and reception rooms and that total was the number of people that that house had to accommodate. We had all been given a postcard to send home with our new address, and those of us still waiting in the bus were very envious when one of our form mates, billeted early, came out to post her card, already changed into a cool summer dress.

After an early unhappy experience I was lucky enough to be sent to a very kind and welcoming home, that of Mr and Mrs Jepson, who most generously accepted me into their family life. Their daughter, my contemporary, remains a good friend to this day.

As things grew more dangerous in the South, with air raids and the Battle of Britain, my mother and young brother had to leave Bexhill. They arrived in Letchworth virtually homeless and the Jepsons generously squeezed them into their already crowded house for a few nights until my mother was able to find other accommodation - no easy task in Letchworth at that time, when the town was bulging with evacuees, refugees and war workers.

Coming down to Letchworth from Newcastle was a complete contrast. I was in a sense evacuated, not by the government but by my parents who decided to send me down here, and the difference between up there and down here was so vast. In Letchworth, we didn't have to run into the shelters every night. In Newcastle, the local area was bombed quite a bit, even our house got hit. Coming down here was totally different. I don't think you ever heard a siren go all the time I was here.

I decided to leave Ireland and I took up my sister Elizabeth's offer of a job opportunity in Letchworth Garden City. I didn't have any idea of what to expect from Letchworth in wartime, nor could I glean much from my sister's letters. These were heavily censored, so that any reference to the War was well and truly blacked out. I had read a lot about how England was coping in the terrible early years of the War. Nightly bombardments on London by the German aircraft were reducing buildings to rubble, while the city's inhabitants were forced to seek shelter underground night after night, to avoid the bombs and blazing buildings. I was concerned that the town of Letchworth must, by its proximity to London, be a very dangerous place in which to live and work. However having been assured by my sister that Letchworth had up to 1943 remained safe from air attacks, I decided that I would join her as soon as I had the necessary travel documents.

The journey by sea and land was long and tiring. I had plenty of time to consider whether I had made the right decision in going to work in a country at war, with no street lighting at night and all windows tightly covered by blackout materials through which not a spark of light must be seen. The rail journey across England was slow and tedious and the carriages were filled with troops of every nationality. Arriving in London, damaged buildings were visible everywhere, creating a very gloomy aspect, and I wondered again if Letchworth would be the same. Already I was regretting having left the green and peaceful fields of home, but there was no turning back now, as my sister Elizabeth was waiting on the platform in London to meet me. We changed trains for the next part of our journey to Letchworth and I wondered again what the town would be like. Would there be bomb-damaged buildings as in London, and what would a Garden City look like? Finally the train stopped at Letchworth Station and I could see the place for myself. What a contrast to the mental picture of a war-damaged town I had carried with me from Ireland. If it is possible to fall in love with a town, I loved Letchworth at first sight, with its wide streets, lovely buildings, flower beds and blossoming trees, everywhere looked so clean and spruce in contrast to London.

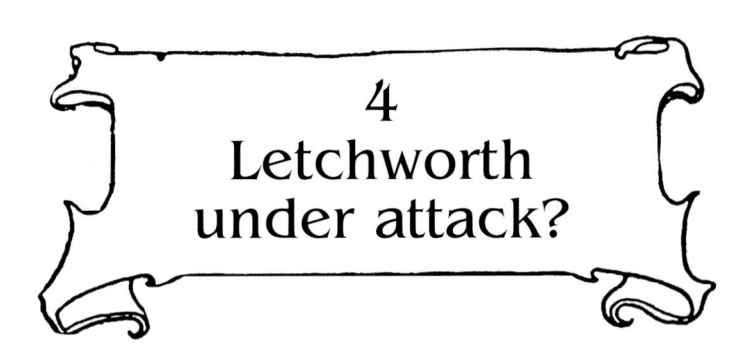

4
Letchworth under attack?

Although Letchworth escaped serious attack during the war, the proximity of air bases meant that allied planes flew over most nights on their way to raids, and enemy planes were also seen in the sky.

One afternoon as we left school we heard first, the eerie sound of the air raid siren alert, then the loud sound of an aeroplane. We had reached the corner shop in Spring Road and many of us children just stood staring in fascination as an aeroplane roared so low over our heads that we could clearly see the pilot in the cockpit. Then we saw that the plane had a swastika on the side and we knew that it was a German plane. Some children screamed and scattered, but my sister and I were rooted to the spot and watched it until it disappeared over the rooftops. We ran all the way home to tell our mother what we had seen, and were very upset and subdued when we were roundly told off for being so silly as to stand and watch the plane. Didn't we know that we could all have been machined-gunned and killed? No, we had not thought of that, but it had all happened so quickly and to us it had seemed an exciting adventure!

When the war started I was at Hillshott School. I can remember things like one playtime we were out there and a German plane followed by a Spitfire came across so low that we could see the pilot, and we did hear that the English one shot the German plane down somewhere near Royston.

I came to Letchworth in 1938, my father was a miner. I went to Westbury School, and later Pixmore School. I was at Westbury School when war started and I remember quite distinctly a Dornier 17 coming over and the teacher shouting out, 'Get down in the kerb, put your hands under your bellies' so we did this, not realising what it was all about basically. I sort of looked up and you could see the rear gunner in the turret quite distinctly from where we were. Apparently they traced it and shot it down over the North Sea. Scary at the time, nevertheless no damage done anywhere.

I remember bomber bases. These 100 bombers and that, you could see them up in the sky. I've seen them flying around. The old Flying Fortresses used to come over in large numbers. Duxford was quite productive in those days, and Litlington, just over the other side of Ashwell, and some of the sheds are still there.

There were many airfields throughout East Anglia and as the Allies went on the offensive with bombing attacks on Germany, it became commonplace to see our planes going out over Letchworth. In daytime it would be formations of Flying Fortresses, but at dusk there would be single Lancasters of the RAF flying over at regular intervals, all set on the same course, but looking very lonely by comparison.

After Coventry was devastated, the Blitz of Germany by our bombers blackened the sky, and after the ritual counting on their return we (all the neighbours) were about to go into our houses again when from the distance a broken humming noise was heard. And then we saw the American bomber limping home with its tail and a wing on fire, barely above the rooftops. We all prayed for a safe landing, and learned the next day that it was safe at Bassingbourn, and that as the pilot stepped from the plane he collapsed, saying he had "brought the boys home". Every man inside the plane was dead. I believe this was used in a TV serial entitled Yanks, which was taken from factual accounts; but there are some of us left who still remember the actual event.

Our War in Letchworth seemed to start with a stray German fighter - who I presume was returning back to base and had some spare bullets in his machine-gun, machine-gunning the Letchworth railway line.

Well I can remember walking down Icknield Way with my son, who was about four, and I looked up and saw this German plane. I was terrified and thought it was going to bomb us, and so I pushed my son and we both went under this hedge, in somebody's garden and stayed there until it had gone. When I had got to Glebe Road and I told my Mum and one of the neighbours, they said that it was a reconnaissance plane.

It seemed to take a long time for anything to happen, until the night skies suddenly became interesting with scatterings of barrage balloons and searchlights. It became even more exciting when, one day after the all-clear had gone, our teacher took the class for a nature walk from Norton Road School and to get some fresh air.

(We had been made to wear our gas-masks while the raid was on.) We were walking in single file opposite Cashio Lane when a German plane roared out of the clouds and began firing a machine gun at us. Remembering our drill we all threw ourselves onto the ground as bits of slate from a nearby house flew into the air. Quite recently I was driving past this same house and noticed they were having the roof re-tiled. I longed to knock at the door to ask if they found anything interesting in the roof, like a few German bullets!

I remember another thing on a Sunday morning. A very misty morning although there were breaks in it. I used to live in Cromwell Road which was next door to the British Tab, as it was in those days, and on top of their works they had two look-out posts with machine guns on them. There was this droning noise, about mid-morning. All of a sudden, right over the railway line which was only about a hundred yards further over, low down, only a few hundred feet up was a black Dornier bomber. The fellows on the Tab roof opened fire at it and we understand it came down in Cambridgeshire. He was hurt, anyway, because smoke was belching out of him. It was either the Home Guard or their own security guards. I don't know which was which, but I know they had a pop at it.

I remember all the barrage balloons, but most of all I used to stand outside school and I used to watch all the Super Fortresses and the gliders, night after night. I used to watch all the searchlights, a long way away.

We came out one night - it was double summer time, and it was quite late, tennish - and the sky was full of aircraft pulling gliders. We could see them as far as you could see, these aircraft pulling gliders. It could have been Arnhem. I remember standing in the Broadway looking up at them absolutely astonished. They used to come over regularly. They came over the night we went to Coventry. You could hear them going and hear them coming back.

I can remember a wreck of a German plane - I have a memory of a firm called Shirtliffs in Icknield Way. Off the track parallel to Icknield Way. I can remember clambering up the fence and looking at the remains of this German plane - it must have been brought there to be cut up - for scrap metal I guess.

Some bombs were dropped in Letchworth, although no real damage was done.

I remember them dropping one or two small bombs on Norton Village school. That rocked the house a bit and there was also some dropped down by the railway line.

They dropped a stick of five or six down Wilbury Road by that big island railway bridge. If you go in the train to Kings Cross and look out you can see the five colours where they blew ruddy great holes in the floor.

They dropped two bombs, thousand pound bombs, either side of the railway up Wilbury Hills way and the craters are still there, white chalk marks about 50 feet across, on each side of the railway where the bridge is.

The two big craters they must have been 40 or 50 ft deep with a span of about, roughly forty foot in diameter and if you go down there today you can see these craters either side of the railway. If you went up there now you wouldn't see anything because they've got cornfields either side. Once the corn's been harvested you'll see them, round rings of chalk. They lay there for some time until they were covered over and filled in. They filled them with chalk and stuff like that.

But I do remember the bombs - Letchworth was targeted. There were two bomb craters this side of the railway line because we went down to play in it - much to our parents' disapproval - and there was also two the other side of the railway line - this end of the bridge - the road bridge. I remember that quite well. So the Germans were definitely after that line because of the K & L, because I think K & L used to provide tanks. I remember the tanks coming through on the goods trains. We used to stand up there and watch them.

Incendiaries were dropped on Letchworth during the time of the London blitz and one night a number landed on the field opposite the Haselfoot houses. Mrs Green (widow of Fred Green the ARP Warden.) remembers members of the family helping to stamp out the flames. As they had come down slowly she remembers they lit up the Spirella Building as if floodlit.

One final memory - the first (and I believe only) bomb to land in Letchworth was plonk in the centre of Wymondley Road (near the Airman's Memorial). The explosion made a great crater and the first casualties were a rabbit and two birds. I took a pretty picture of the scene - but the picture was censored. Presumably as it might have given away vital information to the enemy!

I remember my bed shaking. We had sent Mother off to recoup from all her troubles, and Father and I were there on our own. I was terrified. I didn't get out of bed and get underneath, which was the proper procedure. I thought I would shake it down if I moved! We were lucky. They fell all around. Whether they were aiming at anything here I don't know. They could have been aiming at K & L. It was said that Letchworth could not be seen from the air, because of all the trees.

It is hard to believe you could see the glow of London from Letchworth, but you could. I know one night the bombs were going off so much that my stepbrother had a bed with brass knobs on and they all rattled, and the windows all rattled. Surely that must have been closer. They must have dropped something closer than London.

Considering the industry in this area the town was extremely lucky, the nearest disaster that I was aware of was a flying bomb landing on Pirton.

Doodlebugs used to fly over, and cause much worry amongst the residents, especially when they went silent.

The next ones were the doodlebugs. You could tell the doodlebug because you could hear it whistling. "Here it comes", they'd say. "Under the stairs as soon as the engine cuts out". One of them hit a greenhouse in Pirton. Then they brought out the V2 rocket. It landed in Luton. It was meant for Vauxhall Palace but it hit a hosiery factory.

I remember one night hearing the drone of a doodlebug. I remember looking out of the window and seeing the flame go out, which meant it was going down somewhere. I think they used to travel quite a way after. It could have gone as far as Hatfield, or something like that.

Another terrible thing was when mother, Marian Leitner, and myself were standing at the front door of the Spring Road house one night

'Salute The Soldier' Parade June 4th 1944

in 1944. There were a lot of VI missiles coming over. My father was away on fire service so just the three of us standing at the front door watching these things go over. They came from Broadwater Avenue direction across Spring Road, and one particular one, the fire in the tail went out as it seemed to be over High Avenue. Instead of getting down we just stood there in horror and the explosion blew our hair - the warm air on our faces and our hair blew up. This VI must have landed behind Hillbrow - in the fields between Letchworth and Hitchin. This was our nearest miss luckily during the whole of the War. Although a lot of planes - enemy and our own - passed over Letchworth, we were very lucky that there was nothing in the way of great bomb tragedies at all - that was a near miss that night.

Letchworth really escaped contact with the War as far as bombing or anything like that was concerned. I remember a flying bomb going over. I don't know where it landed. I can't remember any air raids in the times I was here.

One of my vivid memories is of my grandparents coming to stay with us. It would have been either late 1944 or early 1945, and they had only been with us a short time and it was a Sunday evening and I heard a noise which I had not heard before but which my parents recognised as a V1.
We had not got an Anderson shelter in the garden - our air-raid shelter was a solid oak table in the living room and I've got vivid memories of cowering under that. Anyway there were my parents, myself and my grandparents cowering under the oak table and, of course, the inevitable happened - the familiar buzz of the V1 stopped and we waited for the explosion and, in fact, we heard it. We learned afterwards that it had fallen into a field near Pirton and the sole casualty was a rabbit which was killed by the blast. I can also remember just after that time - again on a Sunday evening - when there was a fairly muffled explosion which we learned afterwards was a V2 but I don't know how close that was to Letchworth. I am reliably informed that the nearest a V2 fell to Letchworth was actually over at Arlesey near to the brick fields.

We had one famous doodlebug that came right over, and it came over every house in Letchworth, to hear people talk! One of them came down at Pirton, I think. That passed over Letchworth. The warden on duty at the end of Bedford Road set off running across here, because he thought it had fallen on this part of the estate. So that did come fairly near us.

Say 1941/42, I remember the old doodlebugs they sent over. They were just like a kind of bomb, shaped like a bomb, with two little wings on the back and two big ones on the bottom. The wings were square and there was a little propeller, a motor in it and high explosives. They had a range of about 1500 to 2000 miles and they were basically built to hit a target. The engine would cut and then they would glide for a mile or two miles and then anything that was in their way, that was it. One landed in Pirton, a little village the other side of Hitchin. It did extensive damage to greenhouses and sheds and outbuildings. I don't think there was anybody killed or injured.

They (doodlebugs) were funny looking old things. They made a funny old noise when they come over. We got used to them, you always knew when one was coming. Then there was the V2 rocket. That was a little more devastating. The first one they sent over, though I think it was meant for somewhere else, went into Luton. In my opinion Vauxhall Motors was the target or an armaments factory in Luton and I know there was some fatalities there, quite a lot of injuries, a house was destroyed. Hitler was not all that clever; too clever for his own good or else we would not have been here today to tell the tale.

Planes collide over Letchworth

A major event that many wartime residents of Letchworth remember, was the collision of two American bombers close to the town. There are several eyewitness accounts of this.

About 9am I was busy in my kitchen with my five year old son Jimmy when a formation of American bombers flew over. Jimmy went out to look and watch. He came rushing back saying 'Mummy these aeroplanes are funny and by then I realised something was the matter because the drone of the planes changed. I went out at once and I saw that two planes were in trouble and were coming down. I got hold of my little boy, looked up again and by this time the planes were on fire and were spiralling down. I dumped my boy into a dip by the hedge and lay on top of him for protection. It seemed an eternity till I heard the thump of the planes landing on the ground. One landed just behind our houses in the wood, where it exploded, uprooting trees and shattering them like matches. Luckily only a few branches and lumps of earth came our way but doors and windows were blown and the roof of our house was damaged. The other plane landed further up the lane, killing one woman and a child, which frightened my husband, who was working a tractor in a field nearby. He came rushing home glad to find us alive. We were very shaken for a long time, and we could not forget the sight of the crew, and their belongings, scattered around the fields.

Not such a nice memory was when the Americans were flying in their Flying Fortresses for their daylight raids into Germany later on in the War. It was a lovely bright morning and I was just wheeling my bicycle out of the shed to go to work. On looking up I saw the menacing formation of these enormous aircraft and noted to myself that they were flying far too close together, and how right I was.

As I watched, two of them collided in mid-air and the memory of these poor crew members dropping to earth over Weston will live with me to my dying day. The smell of the collision pervaded the whole area.

One morning during the war I had taken my bicycle from the shed and was pushing it to the road outside. It was a bright day and I heard the now familiar drone of Flying Fortresses overhead. I gazed at them wondering about the American lads who were on the way to drop bombs on Germany in daylight. Had any of them been at the Icknield Halls last Saturday? Had I met any of them when I was driven in an American truck, together with other members of the WVS to the American base at Bassingbourn? British bombers rained bombs during the nights and Americans during the day. Standing there I thought of the German people who were about to suffer the deadly onslaught.

I recall wondering why they flew in such tight formations as, from where I stood, it looked as though they were wing tip to wing tip.

The aircraft circled and reformed into a still tighter formation. They made an ominous pattern of destruction against the once peaceful, clear morning sky. I shivered with thoughts of the thousands of men, women and children who would see this monster flinging death at them from the skies on that lovely morning. The whole force took on the aspect of a mammoth death-dealing machine. Each bomber trailed a vapour wake like a bravely scribed gesture of defiance across the sky, which stitched them together into some sort of mechanical cohesion. There was some sort of beauty there, I thought, if the reason for it was divorced from the appearance.

The powerful throb of the engines filled the skies. Mesmerised by the sight I stood watching.

What followed next I will never forget as long as I live. The centre of that precise formation suddenly turned to chaos. Small unidentifiable particles began to spiral slowly downward like leaves from autumn trees. Then they gathered momentum and plummeted. My horrified gaze returned to the formation. Two of the planes were disintegrating as if some power above had thrown them about like a child with a toy, remorselessly. There was a horrible, acrid smell. There appeared to be puppets hanging from useless strings, lifesaving parachutes alight above them. Some of the chutes did open. The wreckage of two of the once mighty Fortresses spiralled to the ground, the thumps being heard all over the district.

I do understand that some of the GIs at the base planted snowdrop bulbs in Weston Woods as a memorial to those who died on that bright morning.

I think it was the Autumn of 1944, though I am not absolutely certain. On a clear sunny Saturday morning I set out from my home in

The Crescent to collect my sister's repaired cycle from Aldridge's Cycle Shop in The Wynd, Letchworth. Heavily laden Flying Fortresses were climbing from their East Anglian bases and flying westwards, well spread out at this point and heading for an assembly point where they would form up into a huge combat box formation before setting course for their European target.

It was a little before 9 o'clock in the morning when I stood waiting for the cycle shop, to open. Queues had formed in Leys Avenue at Nott's the bakers and at the fruit and vegetable shop at the top of The Wynd.

I heard rather than saw the actual collision of the two Fortresses. One pilot must have opened his engine throttles wide as the sudden unusual roar made me look up. In the direction of Weston, flaming wreckage was beginning to fall. One Fortress was slowly spiralling down in a flat spin, the right way up, but it had lost its tailplane and fuselage just aft of the wings. The wing outermost of the spiral was all alight and as the wreckage descended it left a corkscrew of flames behind it. Bombs, which had fallen out of the fully laden planes detonated when they hit the ground, shaking the earth and the shop windows around me.

Two parachutes deployed fully below and to the side of the main piece of falling wreckage. As the spiralling bomber passed the parachutes the canopies ignited, no doubt because the whole area must have been full of petrol vapours from the full tanks of the outgoing planes. As the flames consumed the parachute canopies the two men fell with the rigging lines and what was left of their flaming canopies streaming out behind them. Everyone just stood helpless.

The spiralling wreckage had passed from my view behind the shops in Leys Avenue but so slowly was it falling I had time to run to the top of The Wynd, to Leys Avenue, to see the last of its fall.

People in the queues were crying. I walked back to the cycle shop, collected my sister's bicycle and went home.

I was not aware of any significant part of the other bomber falling, nor do I know why these planes collided on such a clear day and at a time when they were not in close formation.

I can vividly remember the collision of the two Bombers at Weston. I can also remember how horrified the Home Guard were when they had to go and help clear the wreckage. Many of them were so shocked but to compensate for that I think the Americans gave them the first bacon and eggs some of them had had for a long time.

One of the worst things to happen, of course, was the collision of the American bombers, within the sight of Leys Avenue. On Saturday, 26th August 1944 these American bombers, I have since found out from the United States Air Force were on their way to bomb the U-Boat pens in Brest, France. One of them fell on another within sight of Leys Avenue and they both exploded. Men on parachutes that had escaped from the first bomber had their parachutes all frizzled up and they fell to the ground and it was a most terrible sight for the people in the food queues in Leys Avenue. I didn't see it myself although I heard all the explosions.

It was rumoured that a young woman and her child who had been evacuated to Weston village were killed either by wreckage or bombs from this crash.

Tanks on Letchworth Gate

Tanks were parked along Letchworth Gate during the War. Many people remember seeing them there.

I remember being down here going along Letchworth Gate and you had a tank trap and as you go out of Letchworth Gate either side was sort of built up concrete sides where the tanks used to park there. They were probably parking because some of them were built at K and L (or Jones Cranes). They used to make the tracks for the tanks.

I remember picking flowers along Letchworth Gate and then there were lots of huts and barbed wire so we could not go down there. Afterwards when we went there were a lot of demolished buildings and we did start going again.

My father had a little child's saddle on his cross-bar and he used to cycle me around and I can remember on several occasions being taken up Letchworth Gate which, of course, was a tank park prior to the Normandy invasion. I only have vague recollections of that - my interest in military things has grown over the years and I regret I did not take more interest then but of course, I was only a child of four or five.

There were tanks in Letchworth Gate during the war. One of my worst experiences was while the tanks were coming through. My friends Ken, Ron and I took Mrs Blows' dog, Bob, from Jackmans Place recreation ground, for a walk over the fields. The dog came with us because we played with it, and we took it all over the fields back of Resilia Sports field all the way round to Baldock and went back on the old Great North Road. We came out onto the main road and tanks in an Army convoy came by. The dog was barking at the wheels. We went down Weston Way and walked down to where Knights Templar playing fields are now. It was a farmer's field then. There was a fence in front of us, and the dog went in front. We heard barking, and then we heard a shot. We ran round the corner and the dog was running across the field. The farmer had shot it. He said it was worrying his sheep. The dog came and lay down under one of the big trees with blood coming out of it in two or three places. The farmer told us to clear off; he was going to kill it to put it out of its misery. I had to go with Mrs Mynott to tell Mrs Blow that we had taken her dog for a walk and that it had died, so her husband had to go and collect the dog.

The field was on the Baldock to Letchworth road opposite Knights Templar School. It was the field that is now the school playing field. There were sheep in the field from the farm. I can't remember the farmer's name, but I didn't like him very much at the time. He didn't give the dog a chance to disappear out of the field. He just shot it. I don't think it touched the sheep, but they get worried. They might be in lamb or something like that. That was one of my worst experiences as a kid. I was about twelve or thirteen

During the war Letchworth Gate was all blocked off, because the Army was up there, and tanks. I used to go to St Paul's Church and get my book stamped and sometimes I used to stay to Sunday School and sometimes I used to like going up to see the soldiers and the tanks. I used to go up Letchworth Gate there. I was christened at St Paul's.

I can remember the tanks on Letchworth Gate very vividly, as a child I used to go up there quite a lot and watch them performing and such. There must have been 30 tanks up there, 15 either side.

Wartime Communications

Carrier pigeons were used for taking messages.

There was a mobile pigeon loft. This chap looked after the carrier pigeons. They used to tie a kind of lightweight canister on their leg, with a little cap over the top, so the message couldn't come out. They used to take them and release them and send messages all over the shop. They went to France, Belgium and Holland. That was a way of communicating with the army. In those days there were no such things as phones, airmail or sophisticated things like computers, like we have now. So the pigeons did the job for them.

Americans in Letchworth

With American Air Force bases in the area, there was inevitably interaction between the people of Letchworth and the airmen.

There were some enormous American Air Force stations near here. There were all the fighter bases up around Royston, Bassingbourn, etc.

I remember being down the White Horse at Baldock one night and there was a load of Americans in there when I was. There were about four of us English blokes in there and all of a sudden the Americans started a bit of a ruckus among themselves and within minutes the

American Military Police came and sorted them all out and took them away in trucks. That's all I remember about them. The 'Snowdrops' were wicked. They used to clout you without looking, with sticks this long.

The American Military Police were always up and down in their Jeeps, four to a Jeep, followed by two armoured trucks they could bung them in.

We found that, being an age when the boys had to join up, life was rather strange because suddenly they were away and then we got these foreign servicemen coming into the town on various occasions. There was a Ball for the Free French I remember and then, of course, the Americans arrived and were stationed at Bassingbourn.

Of course, one of the delights for me was standing at the top of my road, Monklands, because Icknield Way ran by and we were very close to the Wilbury Hotel. Now the Wilbury Hotel was a popular watering hole for American servicemen - particularly from Bassingbourn - and I can remember that if they walked by with a girl on their arm it was pretty certain that you could go up and say "Got any gum chum?" and you would get either a stick of chewing gum - or if they were really in a good mood you would get a packet of it. But you never tried it - or very rarely tried it - if they were on their own. It was much better if they were with a girl. They were out to impress the girl - impress them with their generosity - so in that way we got a regular supply of chewing gum.

Cracking the Enigma Code

The "Bombe" code breaking machine was built in Letchworth, but those working on it had no idea what they were building, or what the eventual significance would be. The Bombe, designed by Alan Turing and built by the then British Tabulating Machine Co (later ICL), was used to crack the Enigma Cipher.

The "Tab" Bombes were built by BTM at Letchworth under the leadership of H.H. (Doc) Keen where they were more commonly known as Cantab machines. At least 200 of the 1 ton machines were built. They were over 7' long, 6'6" high and 2' deep and were produced throughout the five year period of the war.

Final assembly took place in the main BTM factory in Icknield Way. This factory later became known as 1/1. Sub-assemblies for the Bombes, including the frames were produced at other Letchworth factories -- wiring at Spirella and engineering of the drums and other parts in the basement of the Ascot, Government Training Centre in Pixmore Avenue.

The 'Bombe' code breaking machine, built in Letchworth by the British Tabulating Machine Co., and used to crack the Enigma Cipher

Security was deliberately kept very low key. New Bombes were collected from the main factory loading ramp, visible from the main road, by a single soldier with an army lorry. He then set off to Bletchley Park or one of the Out-Stations without any form of escort! Nobody took any notice.

To give some idea of the importance of this machine to the allies, the following quote came from the diploma given to all BTM employees who worked on the Bombe when the war in Europe ended.

"It will be gratifying to you to know that His Majesty's Lords Commissioners of the Admiralty have expressed their appreciation of the rapid and efficient production of the Cantab equipment which has materially assisted in the successful prosecution of the war."

This story nearly had a different ending. In about 1943, a Lightning fighter, fitted with fuel pods to extend its range, accidentally dropped one of its 7 foot long, 1 foot diameter pods within 20 to 30 feet of the BTM factory. The pod ruptured and fuel spilled out. Fortunately, the fuel disappeared into the drains without igniting. Had it been a few feet over, it would have landed on the factory area where they were testing the Bombes. The sparks from the relays and rotating drums would have ignited the fuel and probably destroyed the factory.

I worked at the British Tabulating Company in Icknield Way during the war years. I worked there from 1941 to 1945, in the section known as the Engineers Department. They were taking on people, and the area expanded from the ground floor. A long room was built above this and ran parallel with Cromwell Road on the end of the building. Upwards of 100 girls worked there on benches doing wiring work.

Some made cables on frames. My own work was putting connecting wires on to drums, which on the opposite side had rows of wire brushes, and girls had to make sure these were lying flat and level to make a good connection, as they spun round on the "Bombe".

I recall we were rushed down to the air-raid shelter when the siren went on one occasion, apparently Lord Haw-Haw had threatened the Letchworth area from some attention by the Luftwaffe! But that was the only time I remember that happened.

Mr Simisfer was the manager of the whole section, including the men on the shop floor. Mr Archer was one charge hand; we had a forewoman called Rene, but I don't recall her surname.

We used to have long singsong sessions to cure the boredom, when we each chose our favourite song; that took a while to go through. This used to annoy the men downstairs so much that they used to send Jack Darge, their foreman, a Scot, to complain. He used to live at Stotfold.

I lived at Clifton, Beds during the war and the works buses ran early morning, and after work finished, if you missed them, you had to get home by way of Hitchin.

Until the book, 'The Ultra Secret' was published in the seventies we really had no idea what it was we made. We very often had groups of service personnel come and had a look round; the Navy, Army and Americans later on.

People from Bletchley (the boffins) also visited downstairs where the complete Bombe was built. But of course we had no idea who they were or where they were from. There was always some tension about when they were expected.

As soon as the Germans signed for peace we ceased production, all the wiring charts and information was collected up to be destroyed.

The Labour Exchange (that was in those days) were given rooms to interview workers in, and they decided where to direct the person onto their next jobs. I was sent to the Cosmos factory at Bondor at Baldock. They were making valves and radar equipment.

In June 1942 while working as a Capstan Lathe operator at the BTM factory in Icknield Way, I and three colleagues were instructed to report to Vauxhall Motors Luton immediately, to be trained as automatic lathe setters. At the time I had recently registered and was expecting to be called up for military service very soon. The training course was scheduled to last three months but in fact we were recalled to Letchworth after only a couple of weeks to start production at No. 5 Factory. This was a basement under the Government Training Centre in Pixmore Avenue Letchworth. When we arrived there were only two machines installed and we started work on these while squads of soldiers and sailors rolled in and bedded down more machines daily. This was before the days of forklift trucks and machine tools had to be manhandled and rolled in on round steel bars. The basement was very basic, and most of the plumbing and electrical work was carried out around us while we were working. No conduit was available so electricity cables were just clamped to the walls and ceiling. EMTAC (Emergency Machine Tool Assistance Corps.) came in to continue our very sketchy training and for the first few days our tea break caterers were squaddies, who told us that the machine tools they were bringing in had been commandeered at the docks, as and when they arrived from America. Eventually our full complement of 23 autos were installed as were all the lathes, milling, drilling, grinding, Capstan machines, etc. A canteen was provided.

We worked alternate day and night, 12 hour shifts, six and seven shifts each week. We were issued with security passes which had our photographs on them, most unusual in those days, and we were supposed to hand them in when the factory closed down in 1945, but I have seen two recently which were kept as souvenirs.

Foremen and setters were all men, mostly locals and had been transferred from the main factory; some like myself were upgraded from other jobs. A couple were former printers who had been retrained at the Government Training Centre. Operators were all female who had been directed into essential war work They came from two main areas, either Lowestoft or Hastings, and were billeted either with Letchworth families or in the huts at Woodlands Lodge in Baldock. The total workforce was about 120 on each shift.

In 1945 about three years after opening, the factory was shut down, the girls went home and I along with others of a similar age group received our call up papers for the forces.

Strange as it may seem neither I, nor anyone else on the shop floor, were aware of what the piece parts we were making were really for. We were under the impression that the final product was something important for the Admiralty but we did not know what. It was not until the 1970s when honours were awarded to senior members of the firm that we realised we had been involved in such important work; that we had in fact been making parts for 'Bombes' - the British answer to the German 'Enigma' machine. The machines we made were used at Bletchley Park, Station X as it became known.

Winston Churchill said that this was the best-kept secret of the war and had been responsible for saving the lives of many Allied Servicemen and had shortened the war by many years.

The war ends

When the end of the war came in 1945 there were great celebrations in Letchworth, as there were everywhere else in the country.

Eventually on the evening of 7th May 1945 great news of the German surrender was announced. It was very hard to take in, especially for a 15 year old girl like me who half of her life seemed to have been spent at war, with rationing and blackouts and everything like that. The next two days were announced as public holidays. It was very strange to see our fathers at home in the week with nothing to do. I went down to the church that I attended, St. Michael's Church, which was at that time opposite the paddling pool in Norton Way South. Our Rector, Father Hudson, gave thanks for our deliverance, and back home for lunch. At three o'clock the Prime Minister - the great Mr. Churchill - made the declaration of peace on the radio from the Admiralty building. His speech was short but in his usual stirring and sincere way he made a very deep impression. The King also spoke to us over the radio that day.

In the evening my mother and father and I went with some of the other wartime firemen and their wives and families to a big bonfire outside the Spirella building, opposite the old main entrance. We sang and danced. Some of the firemen got on to the fire engine and drove all round Letchworth ringing the bell. Afterwards we walked home to Spring Road, along Broadwater Avenue and although all the street lamps were out of order, of course, I remember being quite nervous at seeing the lights from the houses in Broadwater Avenue streaming out into the street. I could not believe that this was safe after six long years of blackout.

Then on VE day, some of we day girls went back to St. Francis' College in the afternoon where we and nearly all the older boarders went to the Broadway Cinema and saw a crazy Hollywood musical called "Bowery to Broadway". On the newsreel we saw the horrific film of the prisoners in Belsen and Buchenwald - the two camps that the British Army had recently liberated. We felt very sobered down then. Back home I remember my mother had made a jelly for tea and she had opened a tin of highly prized rationed fruit. But amidst our joy we felt very sorry for the many families we knew whose sons and husbands would not be coming home to Letchworth as they had been killed in the War - quite a few from Spring Road. I went to St. Francis' in the evening again where there was another big bonfire - the boarders goose-stepped down the playing field with an effigy of Hitler and he came to his sticky end on the bonfire with us all yelling

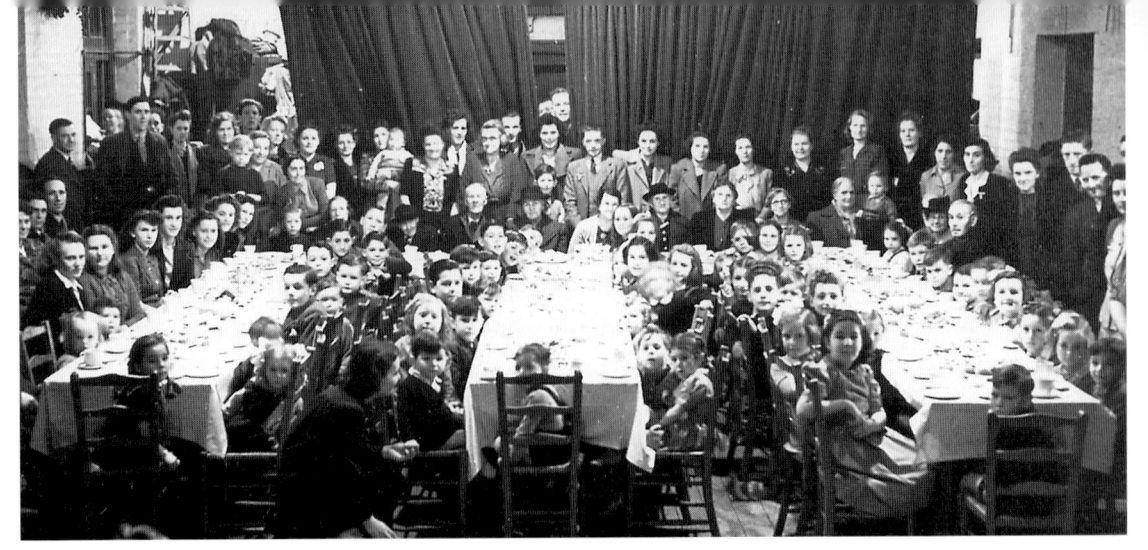

Peace Party at Howard Hall

"Rule Britannia" and other patriotic songs. Thus ending two memorable days in history.

The war with Germany ended May 1945. We celebrated at St. Francis' College. Flags were outside the entrance. The nuns were very happy, as they were Belgian and French.

Sometime during this summer we had a street party to celebrate the end of the war. I still have photographs of us all at the tables. My aunt and cousins who lived in the next road were there as well, amongst the bunting and the jellies.

I was abroad on VE day. We came back into Victoria. We brought everything with us, full kit, rifle, all the lot. We got a taxi from Victoria to Kings Cross, two of us. We got out and asked the driver how much. He said you have done enough for us, boys, this is on me. So we had a free taxi ride across London. So we got on the train and I think we got back into Hitchin. It was the milk train going north and we got as far as Hitchin at five o'clock in the morning and I got out because I was the only one for this area and I had full kit, rifle and the whole damn lot. I walked from Hitchin station and I got as far as Letchworth Police Station and thought sod this for a game. I left my kit bag there, just brought my rifle home and went to Cromwell Road and my Dad was most surprised to see me walk in at six o'clock in the morning.

When the war ended I remember dancing and singing in the streets. The nicest thing I can remember about the War was my Mum waking us up to tell us the War is over and telling us to get up and get dressed as we are going out - make sure you are warm. She took us to the Spirella which had then got the lights up - it was the first we had ever seen it all lit up.

To me, that was like magic. We had never seen floodlights before. To see the building all lit up, we thought it was on fire. She took us

Miss Sheila Tinkler cutting the cake at the Victory Ball, 5th October 1945

round the shops; some of the shop lights were back on. I had never seen them before or if I had I was too young to know. That was fantastic. I remember seeing the steam trains coming into Letchworth station - they were fantastic to see them.

I remember at the end of the War when there was a great big bonfire right in the middle of the Arena - they were burning an effigy of Hitler. There were sweets - I don't know where all the sweets, lemonade and crisps and that all came from but they did They flowed as if there had never been a war. That was a fantastic night that was - well it went on all day. Some people didn't go home, I don't think. There were all the searchlights from various buildings.

I can remember the VE Day celebrations. There were a lot of celebrations on the Arena - particularly the car park, if my memory serves me correct. There was a sort of prefabricated restaurant on the grass area and I can always remember someone riding around on a horse dressed as Adolf Hitler with the familiar slick of hair and moustache and a swastika on their arm. We also had a street party down Monklands and my abiding memory of that is that someone tried to make ice-cream but the overall effect was a taste of burnt custard. We had a sports event which was on the stretch of land between Monklands and Bursland.

On May 8 1945, VE Day, I went with a friend to London, to join in the celebrations, but as I came out of Letchworth station in the evening I was attracted by lights and singing coming from the end of Eastcheap. There I found a crowd gathered on the Arena - then undeveloped with just a grassy area beside the car park - where a great bonfire had been lit. Someone had produced a piano - I believe from the Fire Station, which was then just opposite, in Eastcheap - and community singing was in full swing. My most vivid memory is that of a soldier wearing the slouch hat of the 14th Army, who took the stand to urge the crowd not to forget the men still fighting in the Far East.

My next memory is regarding the end of the war, VE day. The end of the war with Germany, on the 8th May 1945 and a special service was held on the steps of what is now the Town Hall, then the Council Offices, a special service conducted by the Rector of Letchworth, Father Frank Thatcher. The Salvation Army band was asked to play the music for the hymns for that morning so I mingled with the crowd on that occasion. One of the outstanding memories is that after this service which was about twenty minutes to half an hour in duration, the Salvation Army band left from the front of the Council Offices and marched down Eastcheap, towards our building in Norton Way playing the tune 'Rule Britannia'.

I can remember a street party. We had one in Broughton Hill, and Pix Road joined forces. All the neighbours provided different things - bag of sugar, margarine - to do the baking as things were rationed. Sweets were on ration too.

The Salvation Army Senior Band 1943/44. Members of the Young People's Band helped replace men serving in the forces.

On Victory in Europe day many people gathered on the area that is now the Arena Parade, and we all went crazy that night.
Later, residents of Grange Road, Orchard Way and Lammas Way gave a street party, a piano being put in the road with someone banging out suitable tunes. We were joined by some of the blue suited war wounded who were being treated at Fairfield Hospital.

I remember VE night and VJ night. We went on the old fire tenders all round the streets, and we sat on the old fire tenders. They didn't go very fast. It was great for us at ten mile an hour. We thought it was marvellous, It was because the War was over. We had street parties, and all that sort of thing. We had bonfires and roasted potatoes. That was in Spring Road at the time, right at the bottom. The houses and gardens in Spring Road used to back on to the Broadwater Avenue gardens and a big crowd of us had this bonfire up there. We had fireworks and a little sing song you know, 'Bless 'em all' and 'Pack up your old kit bag'.

When the war ended a street party was arranged on the green in Hallmead. The women all brought out tables and chairs and their precious rations, and we celebrated with a fancy dress competition and great relief that the War was over. However, it took a long time for daily life to change very much; rationing continued for another ten years.

At the beginning of June 1945, the war ended in Europe. People were out in the streets waving their Union Jacks, factories closed and everyone was heading for London where the entire population was out enjoying themselves after six years of bombs, air raid warnings, and sleeping in underground shelters.
With several friends, we waited for what seemed hours at Letchworth station for a train to London, and each train that stopped was packed to capacity and we were unable to get on, so we decided to celebrate in Letchworth and Hitchin instead. Bells were ringing for the first time in six years. We had music and dancing on the Arena and later took a bus to Hitchin where there were people dancing in the streets with a great sense of relief and happiness that the long war was finally over. Church bells were ringing out and now our thoughts were on peacetime in England which many people, including myself, had never known.
I bumped into an old Letchworthian recently whom I had not seen for many years. I used to do a great deal of singing when I was young, both solo and with a Concert Party based at Baldock entitled the "Wotsanames", and this old acquaintance was a compere at the local dances. He laughingly said "The last time I saw you, you were singing Land of Hope and Glory on top of the fire station, on VJ night!" If you had any talent at all then you were called upon to use it. We

toured Army camps with our shows, did pantomime at town halls and theatres, and for some of us younger ones life was not all bad. On VE night, someone brought a piano by lorry onto the meadow next to the town car park and put me on top to sing from ten until two o'clock in the morning. The war was over and no-one knew what to do. A crowd of us had been giving a concert at the Youth Club and was still dressed in our costumes. We were going home when someone shouted "The war is over!" So we marched through the silent town singing, and discovered a few people by the car park. Someone lit a bonfire and then the piano turned up. All I remember was seeing the hands of the clock on the town hall going round and thinking my Father would kill me when I got home. I learned later that he was one of the audience, having been on Warden duty.

In aid of the Lord Mayor of London's Flood Relief Fund

★

ST. FRANCIS' THEATRE
SATURDAY, MAY 10
(organized by 12B Company Home Guard Club)

The Wotsanames

a talented company of 25 artists in

Non-Stop Variety

presented by Vera O'Brien

Commencing at 8 p.m.   Early Doors 7.30 p.m.
Tickets 5/-, 3/6 and 2/- obtainable from: Guest's Corn Stores, 112 Norton Way; St. John Ryan, The Arcade; Mr. S. Thacker, 58 Leys Avenue; Ward's Stores, Spring Road and Pixmore Avenue. Ticket-holders guaranteed seats till 8.15 p.m.
Children half price to all seats

'Wotsanames' in 1947

5
Life after the war

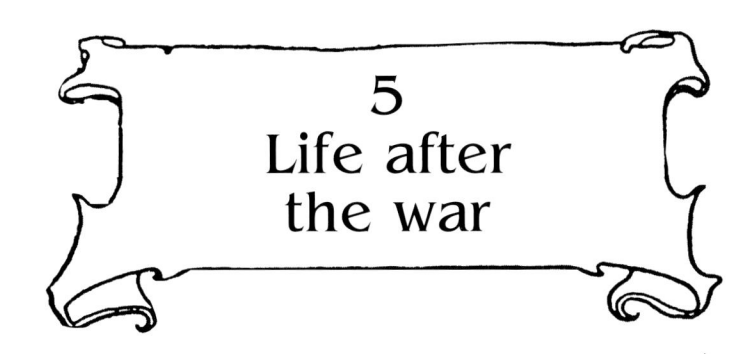

When the War ended there were inevitably changes in Letchworth. Absent husbands returned and rationing eventually ended.

Life began to pick up in Letchworth. The War had ended and we could travel about more easily with more money to spend. We were allowed to walk through the Common to the outdoor swimming pool on our own. My sister and I both had season tickets and soon learnt to swim. We joined the swimming club on Tuesday nights, run by Fred Scott and Margaret Pooley.

We always had plenty to do, so television didn't feature too much in my life. I took Sunday School class at St George's, Norton for some years until my marriage. Work and social life dominated until I started a family.

My first child was born in 1958, I had another in 1959, and my last in 1960.

We went to Munt's in Eastcheap and bought some roller skates which gave us hours of pleasure up and down the roads near home. A fish and chip van started to come round at a regular time and evening. The man would ring a handbell and we would buy ourselves a bag of chips. I think the van was called Saunders and I believe it came from Stotfold.

From 1957 to 1960 I lived in a small flat with an old boiler in the kitchen, under the draining board. I had to lay flat on my stomach with a lighted taper to start the boiler on wash days. There was a small mangle outside to squeeze the excess water out of the clothes before they were hung on the line in the small garden.

Letchworth had changed - it was now much bigger with lots of new homes and the doctors' surgeries were very stretched. It was difficult to get the doctor to visit when your child was sick. I bought a small car, an old Morris Minor convertible, to help me get around with three small children at the end of 1960. We had a bad winter and the car would get stuck in the snow and had to be dug out often.

I had joined the bustling Settlement and Letchworth Art Society as painting was something I could do when my little family were asleep.

We went on holiday to the seaside, Yarmouth, where I remember my mother wearing a long flared dress, it was called the 'New Look'. We enjoyed the sand and sea, especially the rides on the donkeys and around the town on a horse and carriage.

Then one day my father came home with a car, I think it was the first in our road, we were very excited. It was black and shiny with lovely smelling leather upholstery and huge headlamps. It had to be started with a handle in the front, and the side doors opened from the windscreen edge. This opened up our lives, we visited relations we had rarely seen and went on outings to places new.

In the next winter snows we would go to the Roman Camp at Wilbury and snowball with our friends. Father had made us a super sledge with shiny copper runners which gave us hours of fun tobogganing down the steep sides of the camp. It was a real playground for us all; we had hours of fun.

In the spring we would walk down to the railway crossing at Cadwell to watch the trains and stand in the ice cold stream catching tadpoles in our jam jars to take to school. The jars had string handles and often the swinging as we walked would mean that the tadpoles were a bit short of water by the time we arrived home.

Letchworth started to change after the War. Flats were built at the top of Station Road. Hall's Chemist, Soanes' - another sweet shop - came, and then Burton's Building was built and we had the advent of a 50 shilling tailors in the town with a Billiard Saloon above. I can remember the coal shortage in 1947 - we had oil lamps in the shop and my Mother would fill hot-water bottles and put them on the counter so that we could keep our hands warm. As a young girl there was much to do in Letchworth - dances at the Co-op Hall. The

Coach outing in 1948

Spirella had dances once a fortnight – old-fashioned one time and then the next time modern - and we always had very good refreshments provided in the canteen. The Thurstons Fair used to come on the Arena. I think it used to come about twice a year. We played tennis on the Common and, as I say, we had our pictures. Then we would finish up the evening with coffee and chunks of apple pie at Nott's Snack Bar which had opened in Eastcheap. Many a Dinner and Dance for the Chamber of Trade and other organisations were held at the Icknield Halls with Mr. Ralph Nott in charge and the Dance Band in the balcony afterwards. All these events were usually long dresses and evening attire for the men.

OVER 2,000 lb. BANANAS FOR LETCHWORTH
—and more to come

FOR the first time in six weeks bananas are on sale of the wholesalers responsib for this area.

The 1950s were a restless changing time for Letchworthians, towards the end of the decade. Husbands were coming home from the Forces and one gradually ceased to be shocked to hear of a marriage break-up. New businesses and building started and those who had the monopoly on certain businesses found themselves having to face competition. Whitehead's Garage for instance had the monopoly on taxis, where the station was their domain. But now the councils were releasing more Hackney Carriage licences to smaller outlets. One needed only to own one car to be granted a licence.

Letchworth after the war changed so gradually that one was hardly aware of it as a teenager. There was still nothing to do and nowhere to go except for the two cinemas, the Palace and the Broadway; and the dance on a Saturday if you had the money.

Clothing was still on coupons and sweets on ration. One hardly noticed the disappearance of one's old school friends as they returned with their families to the coastal towns, which were not bombed to the same dreadful obliteration of their homes as those in the cities, especially London and Coventry. Many other people remained however; those who had come here from the North to work in munitions had fallen in love with Ebenezer Howard's dream Garden City with its lovely walks and greenery and the gardens.

When the fifties came the memories of the last decade were still strong. It took a while to get used to not having to be prepared for the sirens to go; or to count the bombers at night as they went out on their raids over enemy territory, and then to be awakened in the early hours of morning to count how many had returned.

I first came to Letchworth in 1945 - the end of 1945, just after the War ended. I was just out of the Air Force, and my husband was waiting to be demobbed. When I first came the first thing that struck me about Letchworth was how lovely and quiet it was: the tree-lined streets, and everywhere with gardens. I came from an old town in Kent, and it was so totally different. I wasn't sure whether I was going

George Bourne, Haulage Contractor, with prisoner of war in 1947

to like it to start with - it was so quiet - but it was a marvellous place to bring children up. My husband had moved from Wales in 1934 and he was living here. I met him during the war. We came back to live here because he worked at Marmet. The streets, the stores, the shops - there was something of everything. It was so wide, so spacious, and to someone coming from an old town - I had been in some old towns during the war - it was quite different.

I was working at the Spirella Company in Letchworth during 1953. In fact, I got married in September 1953 whilst working at Spirella, at the ripe old age of 20 years. In those days we did not make wedding lists - you were very grateful for any presents you were given. I remember I had a set of three tins on a stand - coffee, tea and sugar - also a glass bowl and other small items from the ladies I worked with. These all went into my "bottom drawer", as I did not get a house of my own until January 1955.

Coming back to Letchworth

My mother, my sister and I had been to the cinema, one particular Saturday afternoon. As we returned home I ran ahead through the back gate to the back door. I stopped suddenly, as there by the door was a great big kit bag, with a strange man on the doorstep. He spoke to me, and held out his arms, but I still ran straight back to my mother to tell her there was a man there, on the doorstep. My mother and sister immediately recognised him, it was my father, home from the War, and they rushed to greet him. I felt awful that I had not recognised him, poor man, after all those years longing to see us, and I ran away, it must really have upset him.

Letchworth Gate— the town's last relic of war—is being cleared

THIS picture will be welcomed by all residents of Letchworth, and indeed of North Herts. It is proof that, after four years of discussions and what is commonly known as "passing the buck," Letchworth Gate is actually being cleared. One of the main entrances

After my time in the Army I couldn't stand working indoors. Factory life bored me rigid. I was there for about two years I think, in maintenance. So I got the sack. So I walked up Eastcheap to the old Labour Exchange and a fellow who was walking down the road said, "Hello, what are you doing?" I said, "I am fed up with working indoors" and so he said, "Do you want a job?" I said, "Yes, what do you do?" He said, "I am in the building trade as a plasterer and I have got a mate who wants the outside of the house painted, can you do it?" I said, "Of course I can". I had never painted a house in my life. So I went and painted that and I have been in the decorating trade ever since.

As we progressed through school, mostly the boys the minute they were 18 were in the Services, and a lot of the girls followed suit. When we came back after the War everybody had to start off again on their careers. But it turned out to be quite a fun time because all the chaps came back - a lot of us married - people were starting up homes with very little to go on in the way of money or anything else and often nowhere to live. Accommodation was at a premium. I spent the first two years of my married life living in my in-laws' house. Things gradually got better.

After the War ended, the servicemen started returning home and many of us got married and the chaps joined Round Table and we joined Ladies Circle. My husband played in the Cricket Team - The Strollers - which was the third team for Letchworth - and it was a case of 'If you can't beat them - join them', so I became the scorer.

In 1952 I won a window competition for Nestles Baby Food and it was the one and only time I got my name in the paper, winning £50 which was a lot of money in those days. On the 4th February 1953 I married and on that afternoon sweet rationing was abolished. In 1950 Nigel Fisher became the Member of Parliament for the Hitchin constituency, which included Letchworth, replacing Mr. Philip Asterley Jones who had been the MP since 1945. Nigel Fisher was re-elected in 1951, being replaced by Martin Maddan at the next General Election.

The Winter of 47

The Winter of 1947 was very harsh, with heavy falls of snow that remained for weeks.

One of the big things after the War was the Winter of 1947 and I can remember that it started towards the end of January and we had very heavy falls of snow and it seemed to disrupt everything. I remember that just before that time the footings had been dug for houses in Monks Close between Monklands and the cemetery. I can particularly remember the Fire Brigade coming to drain out the

LETCHWORTH BUILDING HELD UP BY WEATHER

Direct labour to be considered

HOLD-UP of building on the Stotfold Road estate committee would be pleased to recommend that similar arrange...

pond which stood on this bit of land. I don't know whether it was the effect of the pond or the fact that all the footings were flooded out when the snow melted but they did have a problem with one of the houses in Monks Close for years afterwards. It had to be shored up with great big timbers. I think that eventually they got the problem sorted out. That was one of my main memories of Winter 1947 and the fact that the buses weren't running and, even though we were young, groups of us would walk from the Wilbury area up to Norton School.

The winter of 1947 was horrendous in Letchworth as it was in the rest of the country. The cold was intense and our resistance was low. Fuel supplies were rationed and the shortages of everything went on and on. The discovery of a pair of nylons was an event to be noted.

After the war I left school and took a secretarial course in Hitchin. The first winter that I was at work in Hitchin was at Shilcocks the Estate Agents - I had to travel on the bus from the Midland Bank in Letchworth down to Hitchin every day and back again at night. The first winter was the dreadful winter of 1946-47 when we had deep snow and freezing ice that went on it seemed forever. We stood shivering at the bus stop and we only had the clapped out old buses that had been in service during the War. Occasionally we could only get as far as Harkness Roses on the bus and we had to walk down the hill. Then another bus would fetch us at Queenswood Drive and drive us into Hitchin for work. So we had to set off very early in the morning because in those days you were not very popular if you were late for work. When we got to work we had fuel ration and there was a coal fire. I used to go over to Walters to get the office tea and coffee ration and we were all very happy - we did not mind all these privations because that terrible war was over.

I remember the terrible winter of 1947. It was pretty bad. I think some of the factories shut because of lack of fuel. We were always having power cuts. We had one Christmas in the sorting office. We used to have soldiers in to help us out with the Christmas rush, as there were not enough unemployed, fortunately. At one time we had the unemployed, but after the War there was a labour shortage, and we had soldiers from somewhere. We were working with candles on the counters. The soldiers were tickled pink. They thought there were fairies in the sorting office, with candles. It was quite dangerous, really.

One winter was very severe. We had an extra deep fall of snow and it had drifted against our back door so we couldn't open it. We had to be dug out. My uncle, who hadn't been fit enough for the army, came and helped to dig round the house, clearing all the paths and the slope. It took all day. My mother wouldn't let us out until it was clear, not even with our Thermogene padding. Shortly after this, with the snow still on the ground, my sister and I became very unwell and the doctor was called. We were confined to bed and had turned a funny shade of yellow. Dr Van de Borght, the Belgian doctor, came and announced that we both had yellow jaundice and were to be confined to the house until we were better. He was a nice, portly doctor. Once he came when we were eating some cod steaks, sitting up in bed. He asked if we minded and took a forkful from both of us saying how nice it was. I expect the deep snow had meant him working longer hours and missing meals due to the difficulty of getting around. My mother was kept busy looking after us, trudging through the snow to change our library books throughout our illness and recovery. During that winter we had some wonderful frost pictures on our bedroom window as at that time we only had a coal fire in the lounge and a paraffin heater in the kitchen, and fuel was hard to come by, we sometimes ran out altogether.

The winter of 1946/1947 was one that I clearly recall. There was the usual pre Christmas cold spell which we took in our stride. Snow started falling in the early months of 1947 and we soon became accustomed to waking up to a white snow-covered world, with no sign of the snow having melted from the night before. Householders cleared a path to their front doors each morning. Before long the snow was piling up on the pavements until rows of snow obelisks were to be seen on every street and pavement in the town. There were no snowploughs to be seen during the War, as far as I can recollect. Soon factories had to close down as there was no way that supplies of coal for heating could be delivered. The entire country was covered in a mantle of frozen snow. Sheep farmers were in dire straits as their flocks were dying in the sub zero temperatures, and fodder had to be dropped by plane to keep the animals alive. Things became really serious when the miners were unable to work because of the weather. Our factory, along with many more in the town, closed down and we were all sent home.

Without work, my sister and I had no way of paying for our accommodation, and we had no way of telling how long this situation would last. Together with dozens of other young people in the town, we went round the streets asking for temporary work. We were eventually taken on by the People's House in Station Road, washing dishes, cleaning floors and tables etc. We didn't mind what we did as long as we could pay Mrs Clements at the end of each week. The cinema, dance halls, etc. were forsaken during this period, and we turned up at the People's House every day prepared to undertake any job, however menial.

LOCAL EFFECT OF COAL SHORTAGE

Some firms fear closing down

THE closing down of many local factories is feared unless the acute coal shortage is remedied within the next few days.

Eventually the snow melted, fuel and supplies were delivered to shops and factories and we were able to resume our work once more. That winter of 1946/1947 is one that will always stay in my memory; as there has never been a winter I have experienced to equal it. However as if to compensate for the worst winter I can recall 1947, the year I got married, was one of the sunniest years I can remember.

Letchworth began to recover from the heavy snows. The spring and summer that followed the bad winter seemed particularly hot and bright with wonderful flowers and fruits in our garden.

King George's coffin passes through Letchworth

When King George VI died in 1952 the train bearing his coffin passed through Letchworth. Townspeople turned out to pay their respects as it passed.

I remember the day King George VI died and his coffin was brought from Sandringham to London via Cambridge and King's Cross. We all stood on the bank overlooking the railway line. We watched it going down the line and as it went by we could see guardsmen standing round the coffin

In 1952 we were allowed to return to school late one afternoon so that we could line up along Station Way to see the Royal Train go right past Letchworth from Sandringham.

One day the whole school had to walk to the railway embankment at Station Way and Burnell Rise to watch the funeral train of King George pass slowly through on its way to London.

I remember the proclamation of the new reign by the Sheriff of Hertford who came down and stood on the steps of the Council Offices, when the new reign began. I was present when King Edward the eighth was proclaimed, when George VI was proclaimed and Elizabeth II was proclaimed and a day or two after they ascended to the throne.

Going back to the year 1952, I well remember the day when King George VI sadly passed away. I was then working in the accounts department of the K and L Steelfounders and Engineers in Dunham's Lane, and the news came round the office at about eleven o'clock in the morning that the King had died. I did not see the funeral train go through Letchworth. I had seen the funeral train of his father King George V (who died on the 11th January 1936) as a schoolboy. I was at Westbury School and we went down to see that train.

Festival of Britain

Also, we all went on a coach to London for the Festival of Britain exhibition where we were all given a coin to commemorate the event. Letchworth also had a Festival exhibition on the Arena in the centre of the town, with lots of trade stands representing all the industries of the town. I remember it rained almost every day that year and even for the Letchworth Carnival, when Melody Norris was crowned Carnival Queen.

The Arena shopping area was a big grass area for circus turns and other things. The 1951 Festival of Britain was celebrated there with various things; there was the Guinness Clock which was designed by Rowland Emett. The car park in Station Way was a big field until the Broadway Hotel was built about 1958. The Police Station was on the same site.

Letchworth's 50th Anniversary

In 1953 Letchworth celebrated its 50th Anniversary with an industrial exhibition on the Arena.

The Jubilee exhibition was on what was then called the Arena. This was a plot of grass beyond the car park behind the Council Offices. It was a large exhibition of all the industries of the town and of course it celebrated the Golden Jubilee of Letchworth. Many of our local traders were there on the stand including the firm where I then worked, K and L Steelfounders. This was a very interesting afternoon to go round and see what Letchworth had achieved over 50 years and it is still today one of my outstanding memories. There was a similar exhibition some years later on the Baldock Road Recreation Ground.

My Husband worked for Foster and Scott and in later years he became a director. They were among the many retailers in the town who took part in the Letchworth 50th Birthday Jubilee Fair held on the Arena and I can well remember going up there and helping on the stand. Foster and Scott's, of course, were the well-known men's and boys' outfitters in The Arcade.

When we had the industrial fair in the 1950s on the Arena, I asked to go up into the Palace cinema. I went upstairs and went out onto the balcony and took some photographs of all that. They are quite good aerial photos.

At the big Trade Exhibition held in 1953 I had just started work. I felt very proud that I was still a boy but I could man a stand.

1953 Jubilee Trade Fair
Celebrating 50 years of Letchworth (held on the Arena)

Left:
Sigma Industry

Bottom Left:
Erecting the Guinness Clock

Bottom Right:
Welcoming the 20,000th visitor

LIFE AFTER THE WAR 75

*Top and Right:
Preparing for
the Fair.
Looking towards
Whitehead's Garage
in Eastcheap.*

*Left:
Window Dressing Competition.
Co-op entry.*

Above: Eastcheap

Right: Brookers' stand

Left:
Tilley Bros'. exhibit

LIFE AFTER THE WAR 77

Above:
Munt's stand

Right:
British Tabulating
Machine Co. Ltd'

Left: Foster & Scott

Above: A service held at the Paddling Pool marks the opening of the Jubilee Trade Fair

Below: S.P.A.D.S. (St Paul's Amateur Dramatic Society)

The Queen's Coronation

1953 was also the year of Queen Elizabeth II's coronation and Letchworth celebrated along with the rest of the country.

The Coronation was that year - 1953. We lived in Bedford Road, and opposite us were pre-fabs. They were all decorated for the Coronation. I think the weather was good before it, but the evening of the Coronation there was a storm and all the decorations were damaged. The people had really taken a lot of care to decorate them. I had a mug from school, with sweets in. I still have it.

My mother actually took us up to see the decorations a couple or so weeks before the Coronation, my sister and I. We went to Westminster Abbey to see the decorations. There were all these crowds, and a policeman said they were rehearsing inside and if we waited here we would see the Queen come out, which we did. That was really exciting.

Illness

People remember the doctors in the town.

Doctors used to make the medicine up on the premises. I remember when I used to go and see Dr Van Der Borght or Dr Kies he would mix your medicine up and you would pay there and then. Dr Van Der Borght was a character. He was lovely. He was huge. I remember going to him with a tummy upset and he said "No raw fruit, no vegetables" in his broken Belgian accent. He had two cars, different colours. I don't remember what they were. They weren't English, but they were large and stood out.

Doctors also used to do minor operations. I pushed a sunflower seed up my nose, and trying to get it out I pushed it farther and farther up. My mum took me up to Dr Kies and he said "Have a walk round the town and come back for him in a quarter of an hour", and he did it there and then. I expect he must have given me a whiff of gas or something. I can remember going into hospital on a Monday morning and having my tonsils and adenoids out and coming round in the afternoon and my mum coming and collecting me about four o'clock. That was with gas, too. Dentists used gas too. When you were at school they would come round and look at your teeth, then about a fortnight later you would have a card come. If it was a green one I think it meant you had to go to the clinic. I can remember going there. Dr Macfadyen used to give you the anaesthetic. There is a spiral staircase in there. I can remember them carrying me into a room where you came out after having your teeth done. In early days they used to give you cocaine. I remember going to Green's the dentist. I never went for quite a few years. I went to Mr Green in Nevells Road and he said, "Oh, you haven't been here before, have you?" I said, "No, I haven't been for quite a few years". He said "I can either pull them all out for your now, or you can come and see me every six months." I said, "I think I will come and see you every six months." So here we are now many more years on and I have still got quite a number of teeth. So I think that was good advice.

Hungarian refugees

In 1956 the Hungarian uprising took place, and a number of Hungarian refugees arrived in Letchworth.

In 1956 the people of Hungary started an unsuccessful revolt against their communist government. Tens of thousands fled abroad. Nine Jewish Hungarian refugee children came to Letchworth and were supported by the local Jewish community. The local council gave them a council house in Bursland and this became a Yeshivah - a traditional orthodox Jewish school. The children were intelligent and tremendously hard working, starting at eight in the morning and continuing until five in the afternoon. Then, in the evening, I took them for a couple of hours to teach them in such a way that their English could be acceptable under the requirements of the Education Act. They spoke neither English nor German just as I lacked Yiddish or Hebrew, so it was an interesting early experience of Multicultural Education. Within nine months they all spoke English and went off to the United States.

Then in 1956 the Hungarians arrived in the town after the uprising with the Russians invading and we took in a Hungarian boy for a while. Also we had another boy too - a French lad. He came with a group of French school children and it turned out that he had come from Algeria because there was trouble out there and he would have been sent out of the country and so we always seemed to be taking in children of various nationalities.

Letchworth had its fair share of refugees - firstly the Belgians in World War One - and after the last war when the Hungarians came. The men folk were keen to show appreciation of the hospitality and offered to help the community in some way. Letchworth Round Table were at the time chopping firewood and delivering coal to the housebound and elderly and I recall one Sunday morning in drenching rain the Hungarians helped to make up the bundles of firewood and fill the coal sacks and go out on the delivery vehicles. They had very little change of clothing and I have always admired their spirit and devotion in helping Round Table that weekend - despite the language difficulties!

I can remember the Hungarians coming here - that was in about 1956/57. There were a lot of people came -. I think that most of those children went to Hillshott School. I think they mostly went to live in that part of the town - Rushy Mead, Broughton Hill, Pixmore

Avenue, Pixmore Way, Ridge Road. Most of them seemed to live in that area of the town. I can remember that there was quite an influx at the time.

In 1957 amongst those refugees were a lot of Hungarian Jewish children - orthodox Jews - and they founded an orthodox school in Monklands. They got me to teach them in the evening so that they would get by in the school. They spoke no English - I don't think they spoke German either - they were very bright children. It was all very low-key.

That was the first big influx after the War of people into Letchworth. Before the War it was the Czechs and people coming from Hitler problems. But you see there was plenty of work in Letchworth at that time - I mean you could get a job anywhere.

We had one of two Yugoslav children at the Grange School in the 50s - their parents had come out after being released from the slave labour camps after the War and they had come here as refugees after the War and they settled. I think we had one Polish family but the others were Yugoslav. The mother of one of them still had her number tattooed on her. She was a lovely lady. They had obviously had a most dreadful time before they got to Letchworth.

I remember in 1956 there was the Hungarian revolution. We had a lot of Hungarians here at the Government Training Centre in Pixmore Avenue. I am talking about the main Post Office in Broadway. The evening they arrived they all came into the Post Office and it was absolutely packed out right to the back and some were probably outside. It was really packed with Hungarians wanting to write home and of course they didn't speak any English and we didn't speak any Hungarian and everyone was sort of flummoxed. They were waving stamps about, but we were not at all sure what they really wanted. It was very difficult. All of a sudden I said "I wonder if they know any German?" I had nearly forgotten my school German, but I brightly said, "Does anyone speak German?" They all brightened up and swung round and came and queued up in front of where I was. It was a very funny thing. I still laugh about it because it was a silly thing to say really, because I didn't remember much German at the time, but we coped. They did want stamps, most of them, so we managed to serve them. I think they were dispersed through the country eventually, but it was a very funny incident.

6
The Town Changes

After the War the town itself changed, with new housing built and new shops appearing. Many people remember the town as being a very safe and friendly place.

The Wynd has been a little backwater of the town for many years. When we came there were stables at the bottom of The Wynd and George Humm, who stood for the local Council with the slogan "Vote for Humm who will get things done", had a small factory which produced lemonade and soft drinks. Also Hive Printers had a factory down there. What also amazed me, and a few more members of the town, was the fact that during the War the Fire Station was positioned in The Wynd. The Auxiliary Fire Station that was, but if there had been a fire I don't know quite how they would have got out. Openshaws also had a building down there as well. We also had a plague of rats down there in those days because the greengrocers on the corner of Leys Avenue used to put all their rubbish out the back there and there it was left.

I loved the old Letchworth. You went shopping on a Saturday afternoon in Leys Avenue and you had a job to pass. You knocked shoulders with people. And another thing - you didn't have to lock your doors. I lived in High Avenue, and if the plumber was coming and I wasn't going to be there, I knew the plumber would just come in and do what he had to do. I did not have to worry whether he had taken anything - not that we had any silver to take in those days - but you didn't have to worry.

It is the town itself that stands out in my memory as being so good. It was more like a large village in some ways. Everybody knew everybody else. I was a stranger here, of course, but it was a good place to make friends. I suppose a lot of us had come through the War and had been in the services, and once we had children we met at schools and that did make a difference.

The Arena in the Town Centre was a grass covered area, and each year was the venue for a fun fair, much enjoyed by the residents of Letchworth.

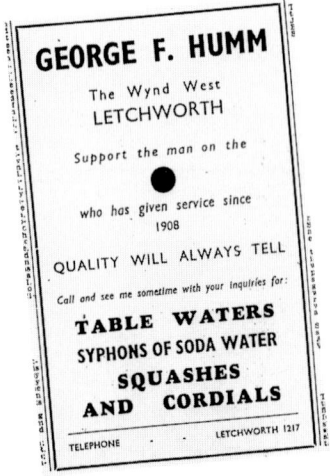

I wasn't here for any street parties at the end of the War. We had celebrated down in Kent. But I remember the fairground on the Arena very much. My first daughter fell off the roundabouts and hurt her shoulders, so that stands in my mind very clearly. I lived over that side of the town, in High Avenue, and we used to walk that way. Then we moved onto the Grange. There were no buses or anything like that. Going shopping used to take us, stepping it out, a good half-hour with a pram. It was a lot further than High Avenue.

They used to use the Arena for travelling fairs that used to come there. Stanley Thurston's Fair was held perhaps once or twice a year and occasionally a circus came.

VISIT
STANLEY THURSTON'S MODERN FAIR
THE ARENA, LETCHWORTH
Commencing Tonight (Friday), June 30th, until Monday, July 10th
OPEN NIGHTLY, 6 p.m. (SATURDAY 2 p.m.) UNTIL BLACK-OUT
ELECTRIC SPEEDWAY, BEN-HUR, ETC.

There were fairs and circuses held on the Arena in town, where the shopping parade and car park is now. We bought candy floss and coloured sawdust balls on pieces of elastic, which we enjoyed on the walk home. I particularly enjoyed the swing-boats, with the ropes you had to pull to keep going.

The green meadow which stood where the shops are now on the Arena started to be used again as a place for Stanley Thurston's biennial fair to be held. There was a small café opposite the Palace cinema where one could get quite a good meal for one shilling and sixpence (seven and a half new pence); nothing fancy of course, just Spam, egg and chips, or beans on toast, Welsh rarebit and so-on.

Housing

Housing was in short supply after the War. Newly-weds often had to live with their in-laws for some years before they could have a house of their own. New houses and flats were built in the town, including the Grange Estate.

I came to Letchworth and we were married at All Saints, Willian, in December 1946. At that time nobody had homes of their own, but it was wonderful because the War was over and that's all we cared about. I went to live with my mother-in-law in Willian Way - one of the most beautiful houses in the Garden City designed by my father-in-law, Wilson Bidwell. Much influenced by the Arts and Crafts movement, it was I guess one of the finest houses in Letchworth at that time, but it was also the coldest - and I have never been so cold in my life as I was that first winter. There was no fuel - food was rationed very tightly - and this house was designed for coal fires in every room - including the bedrooms. We used to go and queue up at the local ironmonger's for paraffin and it was delivered on a bicycle before you got home. If the lamps were kept trimmed you had no smell of anything. During this period we searched for somewhere to live on our own, but it was the game that everybody else was doing. Then the first building licences were granted, so having started my life in the first house to be built in Willian Way, within 18 months I was living in the first house to be built in Willian Way post war. It was restricted to 12-hundred square feet and limited to a cost of £1800. This had to include something to be deducted for the land, which was proportionate, as everywhere in the Garden City then was leasehold. There were nine building licences granted at that time.

I was now in a council house and had been issued with a list of things we were not allowed to do. According to my bit of paper, no tenant was allowed to build any structure in the garden except to a design that met the council's approval. I went to the Housing Department and asked about chicken houses. They had obviously not met this query before, but after a few days sent me an architect's drawing for an approved chicken house, which I duly built. Probably the only approved chicken house in Letchworth.

As I had lived in the Midlands the thing that most impressed me about the Garden City was the terrific high standard of the gardens. Everybody had such a pride - there were no untidy corners anywhere, nobody ever walked over a greensward, nobody ever ran over a greensward and, of course, there were very few cars because of petrol rationing.

Coming from a terraced house in South London, I was delighted with Eastholm Green, a grass crescent with an abandoned tennis court which had lost its netting and, as I was amazed to find, at the front of the green a ditch for surface water between the hedge and the pavement of Norton Road. The ditch continued on west, across

Monklands 1956

the front of Westholm, and, I suppose, ran at some point under Wilbury Road into the Common. Between our house, number eight, and number seven on the west side of the little green, there was an unused allotment. This, when the Grange Estate started to be built, became the beginning of Eastern Way. At the end of our garden was the open fields of Paynes Farm. Occasionally the cows broke through the hedge into our garden. Further along Norton Road to the east, past the school, was Cashio Lane and at the bottom of Cashio Lane, Croft Lane. At the junction of the two was the farm piggery. My children loved to visit the piglets. Beyond the end of Croft Lane was, and still is, a pond, a home for frogs and toads. Later, say in 1951 or 1952, my little son got some tadpoles, kept them in a jam jar in the kitchen, and every day cycled to the pond on his solid tyred unisex fairy cycle, and brought back a medicine bottle of pond water. In due time the tadpoles grew into tiny, agile froglets, escaped their new home, a salad dish, and jumped all over the kitchen, driving my wife crazy.

It was a pretty little semi-detatched house, built in the early years of Letchworth as one of the competition houses. It had a single living room running from front to back. This had the only fireplace and there was only one more room, a tiny eight by eight, that held a coke burning iron stove which provided hot water for the bathroom and kitchen, no doubt considered a wonderful luxury when the house was built in the early 1900s. The long living room had, astonishingly, a mahogany floor. Wall to wall carpet had not been heard of. Outside, a wooden bench was built into the space between the bay window and the front door. Here we could sit out in the summer and watch our little girl playing on the green. The door was the first thing to make me aware that life in the Garden City differed from that which I knew in London. The door was never locked, simply left on the latch.

I moved to Letchworth in November 1948. My husband worked at Dents and because he was on export work - he was on invoices - they got priority over a flat because exports were needed, so as we were given a flat we moved to Letchworth. They were one-bedroom flats and they had just been built in Icknield Way. They were built with the intention of turning them into houses. They never have.

My grandparents lived in Paddock Close, and my great grandparents moved to Rushby Mead. I spent my first three years in Paddock Close. When the houses were built in Bedford Road my parents moved into one. They were one of the first who moved when it was new there. The gardens were not dug. It was just rough soil. There was an orchard at the back, where the garages are now. It was owned by a Mr Scott who lived in Wilbury Road. It was sad when the orchard was cut down and the garages were built.

I think they were mainly all young couples moving in, and all the children were about our age, so we all grew up together. It was just after the war when they started building the houses, about 1948, I think. The houses were on the left-hand side, looking towards the town. I still have the instructions to tenants, advising them on colour schemes, chicken sheds, etc. We kept chickens. My mother used to keep a big pot in the pantry and the eggs were kept in isinglass for when the chickens were not laying. It was a proper walk-in pantry. It took up half the kitchen, and there was a built-in cupboard as well.

My grandparents in Paddock Close had the end of a terrace. You walked round the side and the back door was a big porch, and there was an outside toilet there. There was an open-type gate to the porch and then you walked into their kitchen. In those days it wasn't fitted kitchens, just sideboards. We ate in the kitchen. There was a small room and the stairs went up in the room as well. They didn't have a bathroom to start with, but they had three bedrooms, and one of the bedrooms was turned into a bathroom, about 1960. Bedford Road was all very modern, and my parents were thrilled with it. The soil was heavy clay. Hedges were put in to make boundaries. They had not been there before.

My first child started off at Westbury School. After we moved out of High Avenue we had a little flat in Icknield Way on the top of Abbotts Road. I always remember one night - it was very dark and we didn't have the street lighting there is now, and we lived just on the end of Abbotts Road - I was waiting for my husband to come home and when he came in he was laughing. The flats on the next road were identical, and he had only walked in one there, used his key and gone into the kitchen. He suddenly looked up and luckily it was someone he worked with, who knew him. He said to him "What are you doing here?" The lighting was so bad, I suppose he just thought he was on the wrong end of the road. I said to him "Whatever were you thinking about?" He said "Well, it just looked like Abbotts Road to me."

The Grange Estate

There was a lot of building went on in Letchworth 1950s and 1960s. I did a lot of houses on the Grange, but it was slave work.

I did plastering in the houses on the Grange Estate. I mean, for a three bedroom house you had two plasterers and one labourer and they gave you four and a half days to plaster it, ceiling, walls, the lot. And in those days it was sand and cement on the walls. The first night I came home and I couldn't hold a cup of tea. You lost all your knuckles. It was damned hard work.

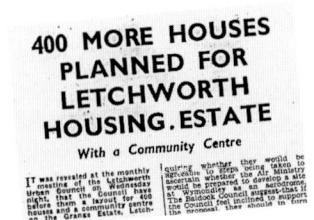

Soon after the War the Grange Estate began to take shape and we moved into a new road called Sparhawke - a fair step from the town centre but eventually some shops were built at the end of Grange Road.

The Grange Estate was started at the beginning of the fifties and we were offered one of the first houses, in Lammas Way. Very well built, with a back boiler fire which worked well and supplied hot water for the kitchen and bathroom. There was also some apparatus that took heat from the chimney and was supposed to send warm air to each of the bedrooms through a hatch in the bedroom wall. This didn't work because, in practice, it did not carry much hot air, but it was useful because it did carry sound, so that if one of the children was crying in the bedroom upstairs you could hear them in the living room downstairs as you listened to your radio programme. In the evening we listened to The Goon Show, the Book at Bedtime, and The Archers, introduced by the phrase 'an everyday story of country folk'. It was some years before we saw television aerials appearing on the chimneystacks. The builders left a long heap of clay from the footings on what was to become the grass verge, between the paving stones and the kerb. We tenants took a poor view of this. You had to clamber over the heap to get to the road and most of us had bicycles. I booked a room at Norton Road School for a meeting to which the council representative and the builder also came. Everything went on amicably, the clay was removed and, as a further result, we established the Grange Tenants' Association, which later became the Community Association.

I lived in Kimberley. They brought in some houses they wanted quickly. They put them up in partitions. We had one of those. It was a terrible place. It was like a prefab - concrete. If you hit it too hard you would go through. I lived there 40 years, so it cannot have been that bad.

We lived in one of the very first houses on the Grange Estate that were built before the war started, there being only three in Lammas Way for many years. The field next door was an excellent cricket pitch for the neighbourhood children. My father took over a small strip of land next door to our house and used it as an allotment, being most incensed when occasionally the cattle in the field (that is now the rest of Lammas Way) strayed into his precious plot. We also kept chickens and after the fields had been harvested of corn we would all go gleaning to add to the feed.

With the War behind us building once more began to go ahead with an enormous backlog of people requiring accommodation. Slowly the Grange Estate began to take shape. My father lost his precious allotment as Lammas Way, Grange Road and the rest of the Estate slowly grew. Under the National Housing Programme building was undertaken under an allocation system. After about four years of marriage and two children my husband and I managed to get a council house, allocated through his employment in a local factory, and we were at last on our own after having shared housing for those early years of not so wedded bliss. The house, in Ordelmere, was large but inadequately heated; one small fireplace having to heat six rooms plus a bathroom, but it was a home of our own.

We were one of the early ones on the Grange Estate. We went to Western Way. That was built up at the far end, and there were probably a dozen more houses up from us towards the town and then all the rest was being built, and it was bricks and mud everywhere. Roads were very messy, and there was a nice lot of bricks and rubble in your garden when you tried to sort the garden out. It was heavy clay soil. The wind used to whip across the fields from Stotfold. There were lovely views on a nice day, but we even had to push in the catch on the door lock because the wind was so strong that way. I certainly remember that we had to get that attended to.

Some of my earliest memories of Letchworth are when my parents, my sister and myself moved from Bursland to Lammas Way on the newly built Grange Estate. At the outbreak of the Second World War construction of the new Estate was discontinued and I remember we were surrounded by fields of dairy cows which regularly raided dad's allotment. We spent many happy hours in this very rural area, playing with our new-found friends, the evacuees from the South Coast who were billeted with local families. I recall my 11th Birthday being celebrated in the newly dug Anderson shelter following an air raid warning.

Grange Road

7
Working in Letchworth

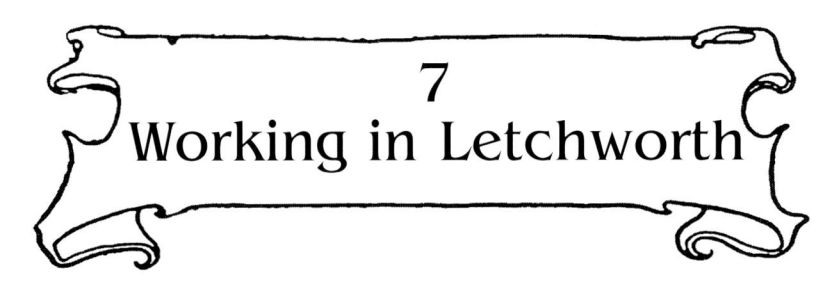

Work in Letchworth both during and after the War was plentiful and varied. Some school pupils had part time jobs in the shops. On leaving school the young people could get jobs in the many companies and shops in the town.

Leaving school

When I was at school I can remember Squires Dairy. I had two aunts who used to work for Squires. I remember Saturday mornings they used to get up about five in the morning and I had to go down to Squires yard. The yard and shops have not changed - if you actually go into the yard, you can see the stables which may have been converted into stores or garages. We had stables there The first job in the morning was to go and wake the horse up, fill the old cart, get the horse out, feed it, back it onto the shafts on the cart and get it ready. Then I used to go down into where the actual dairy was (it was only a small dairy in Letchworth in Leys Avenue). They used to deliver milk two ways, either in the bottle or in the urn, or churn. The bottles used to come round off a cleaner on this thing. There was no automation then, everything was done manually. We used to have a half-pint measure and scoop it in and we used to have to do all this in the morning. It was not just delivery. I used to help them get the milk ready, get my crate, hump it and go charging round Letchworth on the horse and cart which I really enjoyed.

ICL Estimating Dept. staff, 1945.

When I left school I went to Jigs (or Challands), an engineering firm. There was a fellow my father knew, plus Billy Ireland - he used to be a partner - and they were tool makers. Billy was one of the directors. He went over later on to be a director or manager at British Tabulating card printing works, where I worked.
I started there in 1940 and I served my apprenticeship as a toolmaker.

My dad got me a job at the Power Station - which used to be the Electric Company - in Works Road, and I started working in the canteen. I worked with a lady called Minnie. She was a lovely girl and I liked that job very much. She taught me an awful lot. From there I went to Shelvokes, in their kitchen where I worked for a good while. I earned good money at the Power Station −one pound and nine shillings.

My first job was in the CGA. They used to do all milling corn and everything. They had their own milling section. They had their own green stuff, cattle, cows, chickens, and poultry. They used to do all their own gardening stuff, everything. Then they shut the milling part down and concentrated on corn and chickens. They used to experiment with plants. There were two people there, Mr and Mrs Carter. They had an acre or so at the back and what they didn't know about plants you couldn't tell them. They used to pack these seeds and send them all over the world. That went on for years. And they had a big office, right at the side, for administration. They used to do all the wages. Cramphorn's took them over as a garden centre. They moved out, and the Campbell Coach Works moved in. They used it for lorries. My father, he worked in the Sigma, then a place called the Resistor, made all small parts, and that carried on till after the War.
The Spirella also made parachutes, half of Letchworth worked there. Everyone had work. You could get five jobs in one day. I had three jobs in one week. There wasn't a better industry in Hertfordshire or Bedfordshire than there was in Letchworth - Kryn and Lahy, Spirella, ICL. No shortage of work.

I left school in 1960. We used to get ICL apprentices going there (the college). There were workshops in the technical block, with all the machinery. They were on day release. It was what kept the college going. I did a two-year course there, then I worked at ICL. Everyone worked at ICL! My grandmother and a great aunt were at Spirella and my mother and sister worked at Spirella, but I went the other way. I was at a factory which was opposite Irvins, but they closed that factory. I did work at others. My mother said that if you worked at ICL you had got a job for life. I remember the men used to go off on their bikes each morning, up to K and L and that area. You could not get down Icknield Way because of the bikes. You only got two weeks holiday then.

I.C.L. Printing and Stationery Dept., 1960.

I left school probably between ages fifteen and a half and sixteen. Prior to leaving school I was an errand boy for Foster and Scotts - the mens' outfitters in the Arcade. I used to ride their trade bike - very hard work it was as well. So while I was still at school I was their errand boy - I was aged about 13 or 14. That trade bike was still there chained to a cycle rack when they finished only a few years ago. The bike was bought new from County Cycle Stores next door. I worked for them as an errand boy, after school, for seven shillings and sixpence a week - eventually going up to twelve shillings and sixpence a week - four evenings a week and Saturday mornings. I left school although I was encouraged to stay on to get O-levels and went to work at Foster and Scotts full-time. There was a big family of us so I needed to start work. I started there as 'the lad' - an official apprenticeship, so I was very much 'the boy' or 'the lad'. I had to do all the menial stuff. "Come on lad - do that lad". Every fortnight on a Monday stands out in my mind very clearly. I had to put this liquid polish on the floors, downstairs and upstairs. Then you had this great heavy buffer to work it in and then when it had dried you had to bring it up with this big electric polisher. This was something I didn't look forward to - every Monday - it took most of the morning. It was good training though but it was very hard. So that went on for a number of years. I left there about 1960 when I went to ITC. Nevertheless it was good grounding in men's wear, which I rejoined later when I worked at Dyson's.

The war brought many changes and at sixteen years of age I soon had to get myself another job. So, on a Monday morning in November 1939, I arrived at the Garden City full of expectation though I had no idea what I was looking for. I cycled past the Spirella. Corsetry was not among my skills and I freewheeled down a hill, went up another and found Works Road, which looked more promising. I soon came to a tall building, presented myself and within minutes was on the

ANGLIA MATCH CO. WORKS ROAD
LETCHWORTH

have

VACANCIES

for

WOMEN & GIRLS

RATES UP TO 1/7 PER HOUR
PLUS GENEROUS BONUS

47 HOUR WEEK; NO SATURDAY WORK
CANTEEN & ALL WELFARE AMENITIES

APPLY WELFARE OFFICER

payroll of Jigs of Letchworth. Their business was the manufacture of jigs and tools, mainly for the aircraft industry, along with a lot of engineering work for Irvin Airchute as it was then. For the first few months, as the 'new boy' I was often sent on errands delivering and collecting work, usually by means of a handcart. These sorties, once or twice a week, soon gave me a working knowledge of where most of the local companies were to be found.

Moving to Letchworth

Many people moved to the town to find work, especially from the North of England.

My family moved down here in about early 1949 or round about then, but I myself had lived here in Letchworth on and off between 1939 and 1945. I came down from Newcastle on numerous occasions during the war years. I stayed with an aunt of mine who lived in West View, and then I would go back to Newcastle. So I spent a little bit of both during the war years. In 1949, because my father could not get any work in the North, he decided to come down here and stay with the aunt until he finally got a job. The Council provided him with a house and we moved lock stock and barrel down in 1949. Our first place was in Hallmead, 1949 to 1952 we lived in Campers Avenue. In 1952 we got into Campers Road, and that is where we lived as a family until such times as we all got married, and we spread our wings, you know.

My two uncles lived up the North like we all did. They actually cycled from Newcastle to Letchworth to get a job. They went into K and L and asked for a job and the fact that they told them that they had cycled down here for a job got them a job. K and L said that anyone who cycled that far for a job deserved to have a job.

A bloke I used to work with at Morse came from Sunderland. He got on a bus at Newcastle on the way to London. The bus pulled in at Allnutt's café in Baldock (that was the coach stop in the forties and fifties). He had a cup of tea and went to the toilets further down the road under the Town Hall. He talked to another bloke who said he didn't need to go to London to get a job, he could get a job in Letchworth, and he could get somewhere to stay at the Woodlands Hostel in Baldock. So he went back to the bus and told the driver and got his case out of the boot, and walked up to Woodlands Hostel and got himself a job in Letchworth. Quite a lot of people came down from the North to work here.

What my Dad did

People remember their parents' jobs.

My father worked in Letchworth. He worked in Letchworth when he first came down here. He worked for the Council for quite a while.

That was the reason for us to get a house. There were six of us: me, two brothers, three girls. There was only one of us of working age, my elder brother. He started work and I think he worked for a little while for a firm called Tayco. They used to make locks. He worked there for a little while, then he, like myself, ended up working for the old Morse Chain Company. We virtually stayed there until the day it packed up. They were power transmission engineers, part of the Borg Warner set up. The Morse Chain Division of Borg Warner was in Works Road and Borg Warner itself was in Jubilee Road. I worked there forty-odd years from the time I left school until it closed down. They made drive chains for cars, industrial drive chains for agriculture, stuff like that, and they also made lifting chains which went on fork lift trucks.

My Dad was a cattle driver - he used to drive the great big cattle wagons. He used to go all over the place, Birmingham. He would go on the Great North Road, I believe

My father worked at Dents, the printers. They kept on steadily doing their job.
There again, the number of people who worked nights was less in those days. The majority of firms closed for the day and people went home to tea, but after the war I suppose it became gradually more common for firms to economise on their overheads and start shift work. My dad then worked at Shelvoke and Drewry. He used to cycle to work every day. He was gassed in the first war and had a lot of problems in the winter with bronchitis. He was a milling machinist, and they were doing bits of submarines and things like that in the War. He mostly came home to lunch every day, but on bad days he would stay down there and not cycle home and back again. But most days he would come home to lunch

Dent's staff, 1948

K&L WANTED

PATTERNMAKERS
SKILLED AND UNSKILLED
FOUNDRY WORKERS
MOULDERS, FETTLERS,
COREMAKERS (MALE)
SERVICEMEN
UNSKILLED MEN FOR
TRUCK UNLOADING AND
MATERIAL HANDLING

CALL or WRITE THE PERSONNEL DEPARTMENT
K&L STEELFOUNDERS & ENGINEERS LTD
DUNHAMS LANE   LETCHWORTH

My Dad worked all through the War at Kryn and Lahy. He was one of the people who used to run the oxygen plant. British Oxygen in those days used to bring down liquid oxygen in lorries with like a ball on the back. My Dad used to work on a plant - I think it was from Germany - that used to convert it to the bottled gas. I know during the war Kryn and Lahy was very well camouflaged. Lord Haw Haw came on the radio and said "We know where the Kryn and Lahy is", and they lit Letchworth up one night like daylight with flares trying to find it. Once my Dad used to get started on the plant they didn't use to shut it down. They would have blown it sky high with things like that, but luckily they never got hit.

My grandfather used to drive the horse bus. My parents got married down at St Mary's in Letchworth. They came under that parish. My father worked at Whitehead's garage, then at Hanwell Optical. He was in the RAF but got disabled out because he got spondylitis. He was a mechanic in the RAF, and he worked in garages for a while till, I think, he could not work any more because he was disabled.

My father started work in the town, my uncles returned also, and eventually my father and uncle started working together. They were based just off the Wynd, and my other uncle had the opticians in the corner of the Colonnade.

On Sundays mornings I would sometimes go with my father to the workshop, part of the attraction to me was that the Central Dairies next door had four or five ponies stabled there. I would love to visit each one of the milk ponies in their stables and spend time talking to them whilst my father caught up with some work. Above the workshop was Beales, the removal firm, who used the space for extra storage. The man was a friend of father's and did not mind me going in there and looking at all the fascinating books and furniture. Over the other side of the road Claude Hartley kept some of his excess china in a big storage warehouse, behind the shops in Station Road. Claude and my mother were great friends and often used to pass the time of day together while I explored.

My mother used to work at the Marmet in the office before her marriage. I was given a beautiful folder pram from Marmet by my parents. My mother had got a discount because she had worked there. It was an exact miniature copy of the folder pram. My mother's sister worked for Spirella and she used to model the corsets in the showroom.

What I did

During the War many people worked for companies who were producing items used by the forces. Working hours were often long.

We also used to sit and do the salt tablets during the War. They were for the soldiers that were abroad in the hot countries. You had to count out 25 in a little cellophane packet. We used to sit there for hours counting them - but we had to do it - we had to do our share. No such thing as getting out of it - you had to do your share

When you talk about pay, we are talking about six shillings and four pence an hour and a bloke would say "Who are you working for?" and you'd say "Dents, six and six an hour". "You want to work and get seven bob. Go there next morning, put your notice in".
You had to do Saturday morning, get twelve pounds a week. Saturday was part of the working week. They said right, five days a week, Saturday would be classed as overtime. Sunday classed as overtime. Years went on and both sides negotiated again - you work Saturdays, you get time and a half; double time for Sunday.

To begin with, I remember working at Irvin Airchute, and it was a really wonderful place to work. Leslie Irvin himself would come into the factory in the morning, sit at a machine and make a garment or a new type of chute. Now if Leslie Irvin could do it, he maintained that we could do it, and we did. But it was a wonderful place to work.
I worked there until late in 1939, and then was married. After that my workplace became for the Woolwich Arsenal, who had a contract at the Kryn and Lahy turning out bombs and shells. We worked there for two years and turned out four and a half point shells. We had a competition to get the work out on the shifts, and we had a competition to see who could turn the most out. We had to inspect them to see that they were perfect, and the highest in the competition was fortunately on my shift. We turned out 700 shells in one night.
After our contract finished there, I went to work at Davis Precision Tools, who were at the bottom of Works Road, opposite the abattoir, or the Bacon Factory, most people will remember it as. Sometimes looking out of the window in our lunch break you would see a little team of Jewish gentlemen in their black hats and long black coats. They had come to slaughter the animals in their kosher way. It was quite awful to see them, really. But going back to the engineering, we did everything there. We made precision tools, so you had to be able to turn your hand to anything, from milling to grinding, blades, you name it, we did it. We were there when the War finished. We went to the Horseshoes to celebrate.

Being released from the LNER I took a position as librarian in W.H.Smiths in Leys Avenue. There was an excellent library at the rear of this shop with a huge bay window looking on to a small garden. After this employment I went on to work in Bennett's Garage until I married in 1948 and left Letchworth for a short time.

My sister Elizabeth and I worked at Lloyds Lawnmower Co. in Works Road. With the outbreak of War and for its duration, the lawn mowers were put into cold storage, while shells and other types of munitions were turned out in their thousands. The same applied to other factories both in Letchworth and in other towns and cities throughout the country.

One remembers old friends, of course, but mostly I recall the contrasts I encountered in those early days. One day I might find myself in the foundry at the Kryn, keeping an eye open so as to dodge the next gun-turret to come swinging along on the overhead crane. Another errand could take me to the quiet calm of Irvin's packing hall where parachutes were spread on the polished tables. There, I would look at the oak panels on the wall where the names of 'satisfied customers' were written in gold. An ever-increasing list of members of the Caterpillar Club. (I count some of them among my friends but never qualified myself, though a year or two later I spent many an hour wearing a parachute harness.)

Later I took a position in the London and North Eastern Railway goods offices in Norton Way South where I had to stay until the war ended as it was a 'reserved occupation'. Gaslight was still used in the offices and I remember having to work late into the evening under the dim and guttering gas mantles. The abattoir was not far away and I have memories of terrified cattle occasionally escaping and making their way down the line. During the time I was there, horses were still used for collections and deliveries from the goods yard.

One very nice memory was when a Puffed Wheat company were in Icknield Way. You would hear a loud bang and then a lovely smell would pervade the whole area.

I was in the Post Office, and the office was full right to the back. That did not really stop right through the War. It was terribly busy all the time and they used to get very impatient. They were in long queues, and we could not help it; we could not do more than serve. It was very hectic at the time, but we got through.

We worked very long hours. There was a great deal of compulsory overtime, which made our social life extremely difficult. At first we did not get any at all, but eventually we sorted things out, and although we did not finish work until eight-ish, you could usually do something afterwards.

News reporters and photographers also worked hard during the War. There were a lot of weddings to report and photograph and other local events to report on.

There were many war weddings at the various Letchworth churches and in the early days of the War I spent much time cycling from one wedding to another to take precious photographs of the event - the bridegroom being invariably in uniform. Because the film-plates were rationed I could only take one or two pictures per wedding.

Thankfully most of them turned out OK and probably are on display in some Letchworth homes to this day

Always wanting to be a journalist I came for my first job as a cub reporter on the "Citizen" - a real local paper; the only newspaper printed and published in Letchworth. When the War started I had great opportunities due to the depleted editorial staff - Ray Blunt, sports writer, was called up in the RAF and Leslie Bichener, who was editor at that time also joined the RAF. I had to cycle everywhere in the early days of the War. I had to cover local Council meetings, Magistrates Courts (Baldock Court was held in the Baldock Town Hall), Hitchin Guardians meetings, etc. I remember the court agendas always had a number of blackout offences. It was against the law to show a light after sunset and the Air Raid Wardens had to come to court to give evidence in addition to the police constable.

When the evacuees arrived from the Bloomsbury Technical School and Bexhill County School I was on the Station taking photographs. I used a press camera which had quarter glass plates instead of film. Films were difficult to obtain. The usual procedure was to take the plates to Clutterbucks (Mr Clutterbuck was probably Letchworth's first photographer in Icknield Way) and one of the girls, Mr Clutterbuck's daughters, would develop and make prints. When the editor had decided which picture to use we would put it on a bus to Luton - the home of Home Counties Newspapers - where the printing plates would be made and rushed back on a bus to Letchworth. Unfortunately the pictures of the evacuees were censored. I think Clutterbuck's held the plates for some years after the war. Sadly I have no copies.

The Head Girl of the Bexhill School was Mary Edmonds and she was billeted with us in Haselfoot. When I wrote a new column in the Citizen devoted to local youth news she came up with a suggestion for a pen name - "Juvenis". I bowed to her knowledge of Latin and wrote many wartime articles under that pseudonym.

8
A Town of bicycles

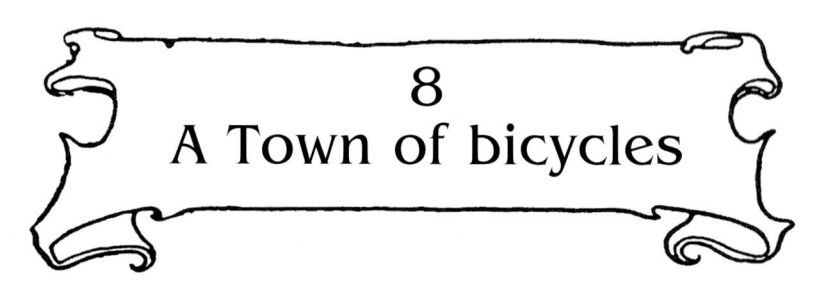

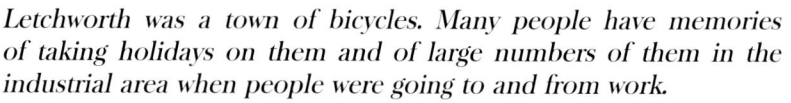

Letchworth was a town of bicycles. Many people have memories of taking holidays on them and of large numbers of them in the industrial area when people were going to and from work.

Letchworth in those days was a town of bicycles. It was a favourite form of transport. We opened at seven o'clock and for the first two hours Station Road was full of people going to work and the bicycle was their only means - or seemed to be - their only means of transport. For the first two hours we were very busy with people going to work coming in to buy their cigarettes and sweets, etc. It was nothing to see 10 bicycles parked outside our shop. Letchworth in those days was a thriving little town with at least seven more tobacconists and confectioners.

The thing I remember mostly about Letchworth is that it was a town of bicycles. A guy came to Letchworth and set up in business. There were two, actually, Sudbury's and Munt's. I think Sudbury's made a fortune. Munt's came a little bit later.

I always remember Letchworth in the mornings. From seven to eight o'clock Works Road was just a mass of bicycles, no cars. When you went to work you got allocated a bicycle space. I remember going down there on our bikes and K & L had an unusual method of telling you what the time was. You had five minutes to get to work because they used to play a hooter. I think they used to start work at 7.30 am. We used to call it the five-to alarm. It used to go off five minutes before you were due to start work. If you heard it when you were down the bottom you used to pedal like hell to get up the road. It was the same again at lunchtime. In those days it was not four o'clock or half past four finish. Six o'clock was your finishing time.

When you were on your way to Hitchin, the road would be full of bikes, coming into Letchworth. They could never get up that hill, Rosehill.

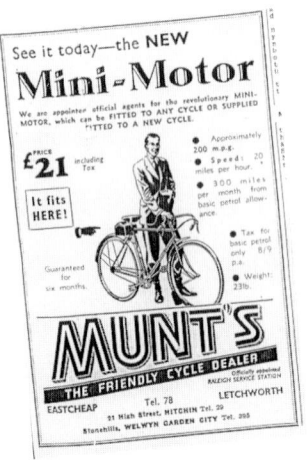

I worked at Davis Precision Tools. There were about 25 of us working there altogether, about five girls and the rest fellows. We were all bicyclists, and at half past twelve the whistle went and we all rushed out. It was about twenty yards to the level crossing. Old steam trains went across into the Kryn and Lahy building, into their foundry, and lo and behold, at least twice a week those gates were closed against us - and under one hour to get home and back for lunch. Then when we got across there would be about four bikes abreast both ways, so that made eight bikes abreast down Works Road, all moaning!

There was a lot of industry at that time - I used to cycle. I remember my father cycling to work along with thousands of others - seething with bikes morning, lunch-time and evening. Not many cars at that time. My Father worked at Shelvoke and Drewry. It was a real bicycle town.

I remember going shopping for my mum on a Saturday morning, and come Saturday night I went to put my bike away and thought "Now where have I left it?" And I thought "I have left it outside the Maypole". I went up there and Leys Avenue was deserted, and there was my bike still up against the kerb outside the Maypole. It would be nice to think you could do that now. Things have changed a little, haven't they?

To begin with all our holidays were on a bicycle. The whole of Letchworth was really on a bicycle at that time and we cycled hither and thither. I suppose everybody in those days had very simple tastes. The delightful thing was that we were all in the same boat. Nobody had got any money and everybody was content with their lot in life and so absolutely thrilled that seven years of war was over - that was all that mattered.

We used to go out on our bikes. I remember going as far as Offley and places like that because there are nice hills there, and having a picnic. The picnic consisted of a bottle of water and some jam sandwiches probably. We also went to Weston Hills. I can remember almost walking to Weston, before Letchworth Gate was officially made.

I remember cycling to Watford with a friend for a weekend and my parents would cycle to Bedford most Wednesday afternoons, as this was early closing day in Letchworth. My friend and I would ride out most evenings around the Hertfordshire villages and I consider that my excellent health to this day was because of food and sweet rationing and all the healthy exercise during my teen years.

My parents would think nothing of cycling up to Cumberlow Green early on a Sunday morning to pick fresh mushrooms and returning with them in time for a delicious Sunday breakfast. They both lived to a ripe old age despite having experienced two World Wars.

On one occasion we cycled to Ashwell for a Vintage Car Rally, it seemed a long way, all uphill and downhill. I wondered how George Revills, who worked for my father, could cycle from and to Ashwell every working day whatever the weather. He must have been very fit.

I cycled everywhere, there were not many cars around and it seemed the most popular form of transport. I would go to my grandmother's and several great aunts, who all lived in Redhoods Way West, to change their libraries and do some extra shopping for them. Everything went into the saddlebag on the back of my bike.

We still cycled and walked around the town quite a lot. I remember seeing Harry Meyer and his sister with the plaits around her head. They would cycle round the town in their open toed sandals, whatever the weather, recording birds and wildlife also the effects of weather patterns.

I got my name in the paper once when I got stopped by a policeman coming up Works Road from work for not having a light on my bike. I got fined five shillings and got my name printed in the paper. That was the height of crime in those days.

And the bicycles, there's another thing. I had never seen so many. Everybody, when work was finished! Now I have been to Holland, and I've seen them there, and when I came to Letchworth I had never seen so many. No matter where you were there was always a bicycle. There were bicycle stands everywhere, and you just parked your bike.

Some people did have cars, but parking was not a problem.

Later in 1939 I bought my first car - a BSA 3-wheeler "Scout". Petrol was rationed but I had a press allocation which meant I was one of the few young men with a 'sports car' so I had no lack of girl friends! There was absolutely no parking problem - one could park anywhere in Leys Avenue or Eastcheap.

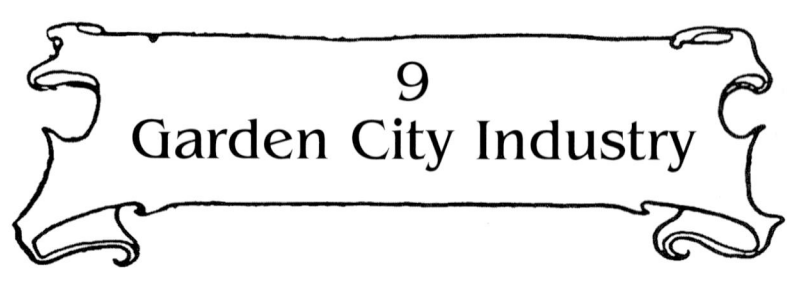

9
Garden City Industry

During the War Letchworth's industry thrived with many firms involved in the manufacture of munitions, etc. Many people remember the companies in the industrial area. Many of the companies were still there after the War, when they reverted to peacetime manufacturing.

Throughout the War, Letchworth literally hummed and was, indeed, a 'hive of activity', for a sixty-hour working week was the norm. Added to that were all the spare-time tasks such as fire-watching and other air raid precaution duties, Home Guard, etc, leaving little time for leisure.

Years passed before we, the public, learned of the more notable work, such as Shelvoke & Drewry producing midget submarines and the Tab's unique contribution towards the development of the 'Enigma' solution.

Everywhere in Letchworth had something to do with the War. Irvin's was involved with parachutes, Morse Chain used to supply a lot of the sprockets and gears for trucks and things like that. Shelvoke's had a big say and all during the War. They used to make heavy duty fork lift trucks.

Kryn and Lahy Ltd. (later renamed K&L Steelfounders and Engineers Ltd.), the 'Kryn' as it was known locally, was fully involved in the war effort. They produced casings for bombs and shells, gun breeches, aircraft components, lifeboat davits, Browett-Lindley air compressors, Cambell oil engines and Jones mobile cranes.

A good thing I was remembering about Letchworth was the industry. I have never lived anywhere where it was all in one place, and I thought that was very forward thinking. My husband was at Marmet. I was very lucky - I always had a very nice pram. He used to do the polishing and plating. He ended up manager of polishing and plating. We always had nice prams. It was a very good family firm to work for, I suppose. The big firms are pretty much all gone - Kryn and Lahy, all the printers, Morse Chain, Shelvoke, ICL - all gone.

Another firm I remember was Dixons (printing machines) and another big factory was Bundy Tubing and Armco. Jubilee Road did not exist until Borg Warner went on it. They took all the left side. Armco took up most of the right hand side.

Railway sidings used to come through where the gasometers are now. They used to go into K and L. They used to cross the road just before where Green Lane and Works Road meet and to go into K & L.

There was the Ascot Training Centre and my father worked there. That goes back quite a long while. People used to come from all over the country to train there. They had accommodation and workshops. They used to run ten week training courses. Where the Letchworth Motor Company is now there used to be Golden Block. They made butter or something. Then further up you had the Co-op garage. They had the dairy in Letchworth Gate for many years.

Another spot I can remember was one of the early buildings - the Nip In Cafe. I knew the two brothers who worked there very well. They were the Drury brothers. They used to supply the big urns and the tea and the cheese rolls to Morse Chain. When I was first there I used to have to fetch the supplies. I remember we had a bit of a treat when we were stocktaking at Morse; we got a cooked lunch at the Nip

In. It was good value. There was another café a bit further down at the bottom of Works Road, but it was not the same. But there was no other way to get food unless you took your lunch in.

Letchworth Bacon Factory was world famous for its pork pies, but if the wind was in the wrong direction it absolutely stank. It was on the corner of Works Road and Green Lane. They used to herd the livestock into the slaughterhouse and sometimes pigs used to get out. I remember I was in the yard of the factory doing something and all of a sudden a massive great pig came flying across with three or four blokes coming after it, all dressed in white and blood stained, chasing this pig and trying to get hold of it. It took about four of them but they managed to get hold of it and drag it back. I would not have thought that it was a very pleasant place to work. The smell put me off. But Letchworth bacon was world known.

One of my memories of that time was the "pig bins" - I can smell them now. Mother used to send us with our peelings and things to Archer's Way, which wasn't far from where we lived.

I also remember the Anglia Match Factory, next to where I worked. They used to put the reject matches out in the yard at the back, and we used to get over the fence and pick them up and take them home. They struck!

There was a lot of heavy industry in Works Road and Icknield Way. I remember K & L Steelfounders. During the war they were involved in armaments, shells and things like that. I presume that was the connection with the tanks parked in Letchworth Gate. There was Meredew's (big furniture makers), Cooper Stewart's, Irvin's, Naco (locks and keys), Chater Lea, Shelvoke and Drewry, and Stoddard's Brushes. Spirella was a very prominent firm. The firms were family firms. There was no power station. I remember the old Morse Chain building, Silentnight (they made mattresses), Dent's the bookbinders - a very prominent firm, and the British Tabulating Machine Company, making early computing machines.

In Birds Hill there was the oldest foundry in Letchworth. The building is still there with the nameplate up on it. On the right hand side is Lloyds who make grass cutting machines. Where Bridger Packaging is now was Lewis Falk's - they made badges and embroidery. The lawnmower firm must be the only remaining industrial plant in Letchworth from the 1950s.

There were many factories in Letchworth engaged on war work. My own company started in Fenner's Building in the Wynd, manufacturing dental brushes and products for the dental trade and held Ministry of Defence contracts to supply the armed forces. After the restrictions of the War, local Industry began to re-organise for the

new era of peace. The Letchworth Manufacturers' Association, which had been formed for mutual support of local industry, was wound up. The secretary was Howard Morriss, a Director of Marmet Ltd.
In 1950 we built our first new custom designed factory in Icknield Way next door to the Sigma Instrument Company. Stoddard Manufacturing Co. is now one of the oldest family-owned businesses in Letchworth and are still contractors to the Ministry of Defence. Today they export their products to over 65 countries.

As I pass along Works Road and Icknield Way nearly sixty years later, I see in my mind's eye the factories that once were there. Going up Birds Hill one came to a small factory that belonged to Foster Instruments, then Lewis Falk's, Lorraine Embroidery Works and the Casting Company with its associated pattern-making shop, Furmston & Lawlor. Further on were to be found Hanwell Optical and two builders' supply yards - Eastwood's and another with the lovely name, I thought, of 'J. Mhur Pratt'. This latter was next door to Jigs, who gradually took over more and more of the Tenement Building, though space remained for St Christopher Press and a small works (Kryptok) banging out nuts and bolts by the million, whilst Cobb & Ward hung on to a little bit of their yard space.

Much of the other side of Birds Hill was occupied by Lloyds, and I fancy I can still hear the constant 'clink, clink' as many thousands of newly-forged anti-aircraft shells were tossed onto the loading-stage. These were brought from the railway goods yard on a flat dray. One of these was drawn by a Kamer three-wheeled 'mechanical horse', the other by a real one, which would stand contentedly with its nose in a bag of oats as the newly-machined shells were loaded, more carefully, for despatch to the munitions works for filling.

Openshaw's builder's yard has long gone, though the name remains as does the Nip-In Cafe' on the corner. (I don't suppose they can still provide an enamel jug of hot, sweet tea for a tanner or one of those wonderful homemade apple turnovers for tuppence.)
Foster's main works were in Pixmore Avenue and I remember Kosmos, a plant making roll film. Further up was to be found, behind a petrol station, the collection of huts that housed the Plating & Polishing Company. At the top was, of course, the Cottage Hospital, repairing a constant stream of industrial injuries of one sort or another.
Returning, one passed the Laundry and the Government Training Centre, then still known as the 'Ascot' from its motor car days. There, among other trainees, sailors of the Fleet Air Arm were taught to be aircraft mechanics.
Further down on that side was the Garden City Press. The prime site on the corner was occupied by Morse Chain, whose production would have circled the globe.

Opposite was the power station with its four huge wooden cooling towers, pouring out clouds of steam to mingle with the general smoke. A side effect was that on frosty nights and mornings it turned Works Road into a skating rink for the multitude of cyclists. Another hazard faced by we poor commuters arrived when the clocks were altered. Lighting-up time was six o'clock and woe betide any whose lamp batteries had been allowed to run down in the summer. The police, reinforced by the War Reserve Specials, would be out in force, 'summonsing' the law-breakers and helping to swell the Government's coffers with the five shilling fines - War didn't come cheap, even in those days.

Morse's neighbours were the Garden City Embroidery Works, turning out everything from corporals' stripes to pilots' wings, then the instrument works of Cooper Stewart and Dent's bookbindery.

Across the road was a company that seemed to produce bitumastic blocks for roofing, then Ewart's Geyser factory, topped by their famous figure of Mercury. On the corner of Dunhams Lane sat the Herts Rubber Company and their neighbours, Boake Roberts, who produced an obnoxious-smelling fire fighting liquid to add to the unique and sometimes revolting stench that often pervaded that end of the town. Close by stood T. H. Dixon's engineering works, offending no one.

The sulphur content of the environment came from the other side of Works Road which was occupied by the Gas Works. Their coal was delivered by rail, for the Garden City Company owned a system of branch lines that extended from the goods yard. Running parallel with the main line to Baldock, it delivered more coal to maintain the huge stocks at the power station and even took a few truckloads of bricks to Mr Pratt.

On reaching Green Lane, one track continued over a level-crossing immediately by the bridge taking cattle-wagons and the big yellow Saxa salt vans to the abattoir, the smelliest culprit of all. Over the road also went huge tree trunks - poplar - to be made into matchboxes by Anglia Match. A further branch swept around from the gas works and crossed Works Road to enter the vast Kryn & Lahy complex. They had their own locomotive and also used an old-fashioned steam crane with a vertical boiler to move the trucks around the various workshops.

The noise of the heavy industry at the 'Kryn' could be heard for miles as thousands turned out bombs and other steel forgings by day and night. Getting grit in one's eye was a regular hazard when passing.

As well as the Kryn, this branch served Stanton's timber yard, then crossed Dunhams Lane to Meredew's Furniture, Dent's and on, ending at the Ascot. As far as I know, all that remains of the system is a post that once supported a level-crossing gate, now standing alone on the corner by the van-hire yard.

My journeys took me less frequently to Icknield Way but I passed Golden Block Margarine and the Hollerith ('Tab') card-printing works often enough. Over the road was Hand's Trailers and, further down, a survivor, Standard Advertising Tapes. The rest of that side was pretty well taken up by Shelvoke & Drewry and Tab No 1, the British Tabulating Machine Co. Opposite stood Chater-Lea famous in the pre-war cycling world, Camco - Canadian & American Machinery Co., Bundy Tubing and their associate, the American Rolled Metal Co.

The Creamery stood in isolation amidst the Army's tank park on Letchworth Gate., The Co-op garage divided Hoy-Whitley (aircraft parts) and others from IMn's. At the other end of the Way, beyond Spirella (who were soon conscripted into making parachutes) was Marmet, Wheels (London) Ltd. and another engineering works, Shirtliffe Bros. Further on, the famous Sigma Instruments. I'm sure there were many more around but memory doesn't stretch that far. My travelling soon came to an end and I was confined to the gloom of the blacked-out factory, day and night, before making my escape and joining the RAF.

The Garden City has grown since; then, it was but a minnow compared to the major industrial centres of Britain. Nevertheless, few towns could have boasted more diversity and adaptability. Letchworth and all who worked there truly 'did their bit'.

Foster and Scotts

Foster and Scott's was one of the gentlemen's outfitters in the Town Centre.

I first joined Foster and Scott's in 1953 but prior to that the company had been running in The Arcade since 1927. It was started by a Mr. Scott. At that time he was also a representative of the Foster Raincoat Company. He didn't really know what to call the shop so he decided that Foster and Scott's would be quite a good name. He carried on with it for a number of years - until 1930 or thereabouts. Lewis Bullard, who had been a member of staff of Owen Wards of Ipswich came to Letchworth and took over as manager at Foster and Scott's.

During the war years, like all other businesses it had suffered very much by shortages, by rationing and by the normal problems associated with any company surrounded by war. Rationing was introduced, I believe, in 1940 and in those days if you wanted to buy a suit it cost you 26 coupons: 20 coupons for a two-piece suit and

Foster and Scott's staff – 1957. (Far right: Lewis Bullard - Managing Director)

the extra six coupons was for a waistcoat, if you decided you wanted to make it a three-piece. However, the clothing allowance was very meagre and that is why, basically, people who did buy a suit bought one without the waistcoat. During the War the shop was the official outfitters for the girls at St. Francis' College in the Broadway. It was always a boast of Lewis Bullard that in spite of everything during the War he kept their uniform going. Not always perhaps quite the green that it should have been but, nevertheless, he managed to keep it going and that he was very proud of.

When the War finished clothing coupons were still required until about 1951-52 and then rationing finished. Supplies often were short but, having said that, if you had a good name you might be able to get hold of some good brands. I came to Foster and Scott's in 1953 to look after the boys and school department. This still included St. Francis' College, and we did a certain amount of games clothing for St. Christopher School. In 1953 there were a lot of menswear retailers in the town which included Spink's in Leys Avenue, Rowlinson's in Leys Avenue and across the road opposite to them Barker's, the high class menswear shop which was run by two brothers - Bernard and Clifford. Coming up the road we come into The Arcade where Foster and Scott's were. Go into Eastcheap and then there was Hawkin's from Hitchin, the Co-op sold clothes, and where the electricity showrooms were, there was a menswear shop called Pugh's. In Station Road we had Wade's at the top and Dyson's towards the bottom. We were all in competition with one another but, having said that, we all managed to make a living.

When I first joined Foster and Scott's they occupied two units in The Arcade and we sold good quality menswear, boys clothing, school clothing, and, of course, as I said earlier St. Francis' clothing. Unfortunately, in 1954, there was a change of sisters who were looking after the girls' school clothing and Foster and Scott's lost the contract and it was handed over to Daniel Neal's of London. Local people were not at all happy with this but the fact remained that they had to go to London to get their children's clothing.

In 1953, in celebration of Letchworth's 50 years, there was a Trade Show. This was on the Arena and local companies and retailers were invited to participate. Foster and Scott's had a stand there. It was a well-received show and everybody thought it was very worth while.

Opposite us in The Arcade was Claude Hartley's China and Glass shop which was a very, very successful business and immediately next to them was the Health Food Stores and next to them was M.G. Bennett's, the jewellers. Opposite Bennetts was Clifford Wright's Cycle Shop they called it although, in fact, by then they were selling basically radios, televisions and that sort of thing. This sort of area was a very good attraction for people to come down and have a look round and subsequently come in and do business with one or other or all of us.

A window display of Foster and Scott in their shop in 'The Arcade' Letchworth in the late 1950s.

Gavin Jones' Nursery

Gavin Jones' Nursery was well known as a supplier of garden plants, not just locally but nationwide, winning prizes at Chelsea and supplying London stores.

In 1939 I had been working at Gavin Jones' Nurseries for three years, then I stayed through the War. Gavin Jones was busy with his Home Guard and his wife was very busy with the Red Cross. There was not a lot to do in the nursery except keep the collection of plants together. It was a big collection, probably the best in the country. There were one or two workers who were not up to army standard, and we produced cut flowers for London to pay to keep it going. We were paid quite well, you see, for peonies and things we sent to Selfridges and to Edward Goodyear, the Queen's florist.

It was after the war that the Chelsea connection brought Letchworth's name forward and all the wonderful things down there. We had the water gardens, of which Churchill bought one. His wife came and bought one; that was a great thrill. It is at Chartwell, but it is all overgrown. That was when Churchill was out of office, in the 1950s. I remember I went down there and he said, "I shall be back next year", or something like that, and he was. I should think we were exhibiting in 1947 and 1948. My husband got a crane and we were the first to use a crane on the rock garden bank at Chelsea. I don't know whether it was from Jones' Cranes at Letchworth, but it might have been. It was quite a small thing, but a wonderful thing to help. We won Gold Medals each time we exhibited. I think really we did because of the size of the garden. There was a man named Whitelegg who exhibited; he also got a Gold Medal, but I think there were only the two of us.

Really and truly, my husband did the designing. We used to go to the Forest of Dean and choose the stone, and mark the stone, the bluffs. Then he knew what he was going to do. He did a rough sketch and Gavin Jones would make suggestions and Mrs Gavin Jones would plant it. I used to grow the plants for it and I used to go down to Blooms of Bressingham and places like that and get the plants together and they would make the best of what I put for them.

They went all through this period up to 1960, not every year, about every other year. It was too costly. I don't think anyone else did, unless they were paid. We did two formal gardens for the Financial Times but that was right up in the 1970s. We were paid for that, of course.

TSB BANK

The Trustees Savings Bank, later to become the TSB and then Lloyds TSB, had a branch in Letchworth. As a former Manager explains, the bank was Government sponsored and its aim was to encourage savings.

The first Trustee Savings Bank in North Herts was opened in March 1949 in Hitchin. Letchworth was opened in March 1949 and I became manager here at Easter 1952. The Trustee Savings Bank was opened to help people with their savings. The TSB was not allowed to lend money - all the accounts were deposit accounts. The TSB movement was a non-profit making organisation. It was Government sponsored and Government guaranteed. The surpluses were used to improve offices, etc. and to pay general expenses. We also offered National Savings Certificates and National Savings products generally.

The TSB introduced direct transfer savings schemes in the factories, by which employees authorised deductions from wages, which were credited to bank accounts each month. We had hundreds and hundreds of these accounts, and they really introduced people from the factories to the art of saving. We also had savings schemes in schools.

The TSB did a good job as a custodian for depositors' money. It could only offer a service, as it could not lend money or offer cheque books. This came later.

The management of the Trustee Savings Banks were rather odd. We had something like a thousand offices, with about 70 or 80 head offices, and each local branch had a Board of local Trustees - all voluntary workers. The original Chairman at Letchworth was Mr George Woodbridge. I think he was Chairman of Letchworth Urban District Council for two or three terms. The other Trustees were Mr J. D. Ritchie (senior), Mr J. P. Knowles, Mr Jim Collins, Miss Kathleen Kaye and Mr Cliff Wright. Then when the TSB unfortunately became a private limited company the Trustees were no longer needed and were not used and the banks changed from that day on. When we could issue chequebooks and start lending money it was a different kind of atmosphere and a different kind of bank altogether.

I lived in the flat above the Bank from 1956 onwards, and my daughter was born there. We used to sit up in the windows of the flat looking out, when our daughter was about three or four years old and we saw old Mr Clarence Howard's insurance company office (which was later used as a surgery by Dr Jaffey) taken down, and then Bennett's had a brand new garage built on that site. We used to thoroughly enjoy watching the spidermen walking about on the girders to construct the new workshops. We moved to Howard Drive in 1964 because the flat was needed to increase the size of the Bank.

As a customer of the TSB it was always very nice to be able to deal with people you knew. We obviously knew the Manager and also the members of the Board of Trustees. The set up at the Bank was friendly. It wasn't intimidating at all. You could go in and the staff were always very helpful. It made it a very much easier thing to deal with people you knew there rather than the rather impersonal way in which banking is carried on today.

The Citizen

The Citizen was Letchworth's local newspaper, reporting life in the town.

I remember the Citizen. My sister-in-law worked in the Citizen office, in Norton Way North, facing the garages, where the windows place is now. The Citizen was all about Letchworth news and Letchworth people - many weddings were reported. They used to tell us where everybody worked, where they went for their honeymoon, what they wore for the wedding and who were the Bridesmaids. They used to give you a lot of detail - it was all the local news. Uncle Ian had his children's' corner in it and used to have competitions for those who joined. It was printed in Norton Way North.

Clutterbuck Photographers

Clutterbuck's was the local photographer, whose house in Icknield Way was a local landmark.

On the edge of the Common, in Icknield Way was Clutterbuck's, the photographers. He had an intriguing, mainly wooden house with a beautiful garden. It was full of models of squirrels, birds and other small creatures, strategically placed among the flowers and even on the roof. We were taken there at regular intervals to update the photos we sent to my father who was stationed abroad with the Royal Army Medical Corps. Later on, we also went to Julian Tayler, another photographer in town. As a child I was more impressed by the Clutterbucks' little domain, and their efforts to amuse me in order to keep me still enough to have the photo taken.

With the photos my sister and I would write letters to my father, as soon as we were able to. I used to look at his photo in uniform and wonder what he was like, what he sounded like when he spoke, having no recollection of him whatsoever.

10 Shopping

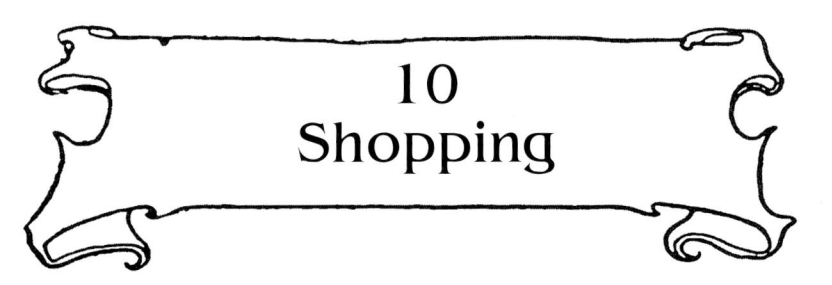

Letchworth Town Centre had a wide variety of shops where residents enjoyed going to purchase their groceries and other items and to meet friends. It was a very friendly and helpful place. Trades people used to call at the houses as well.

We came to Letchworth in 1938. We arrived one lovely March day and I can remember walking up the Broadway with my parents and the trees were just coming out and my father turned to my mother and said, "This is going to be a lovely place - we shall be happy here", and I, and he, were always happy here. We settled in "The Cabin" which was the old Post Office and when we came there were two holes in the original counter where the Post Office wire was put. The garages at the back of the garden were the original Post Office sorting rooms and that is why they have a fireplace in, which always fascinated me as a child - the fact that four garages had a fireplace in.

Burton's building was not yet built neither were the flats at the top of Station Road. Wright's Cycle Shop was next door to us and Bennett's the jewellers on the corner. Then there was Georgio's and opposite, Bennett's Garage, Cakebread Robey's, Wallace Dairies and the People's House. On the same side going down from us was Bugby's - the hairdressers (men's and women's), then Mr. Large with his second-hand furniture shop, Llewellens, Russells - the chemists - Ansells the butchers, then on the corner of the Wynd was the Central Dairies, Franklins, Beddoes and Softly's the grocers; then at the bottom George Deans, the greengrocers, who was a very well known family in Letchworth at that time. Right at the bottom of Birds Hill was Guests, the corn chandlers, the forerunner of the Pet Shop.

Stokes was at the corner of the other end of Station Road with Favells, the undertakers. Berretts, the electrical shop was also there. At the top of Station Road was Smiths - a very good ladies' dress shop over which was the Metro Hairdressing Salon. We were in the Cabin from 1938 to 1953 when my father died and sold the shop to Simmonds.

They sent me out to do some shopping. I went into Hartley's shop at the bottom of Station Way. After I was given my purchases I realised that I had come out without any money. The shop assistant, Ken Saunders, said, 'That's all right. You are Mrs......... daughter's husband aren't you?" And then, as I was turning to go out, he said "Here, you'll need this for the other shops" and gave me a pound note. That sort of thing did not happen in London.

I had gone to Hartley's to get meal for my chickens. This was obtained against the coupon that would occasionally entitle you to an egg. A great many people kept chickens at that time.

Going over to the shopping in Letchworth from those days, rations were very bad but at least you got good service when they had got anything there, and the shop assistants were very, very helpful. After the war there were so many shops in Letchworth it was really a pleasure to shop. Each shop had a chair by the counter for older people to sit down. You took your order in and ordered what you wanted and later that day it would be delivered to your house. There was Moss's, the Health Food Stores, the Co-op, International, Angell's, the Maypole. There were loads of shops. They never let you down, and your order came; it was luxury. Then, getting to the other shops, there was Green's the furnisher, the Co-op again, and for your leisure there was Munts who sold prams, bicycles and toys. But for Gem cycles you went to Sudbury's. These were super racing cycles, etc., and the assistants were encouraged to serve good customers who would spend £15 to £40 for a bicycle, and also dear little old ladies who fetched their leaky radios in with batteries that had been in for a month and not switched off. We would say to them "Walk away and do your shopping, we will do it".

But the town was so busy in those days. That's what I remember. You went into the town on a Saturday and it was heaving with people. I suppose it was before the advent of the car in any degree and everybody did their shopping locally. Because I remember seeing all those prams outside Woolworth's - Saturday afternoon in the centre of the town. We had so many grocery shops - really you could buy anything in Letchworth.

There were about three or four bespoke tailors then. They all disappeared.

Yes. Foster and Scott's. Spink's, of course. My father used to go to Foster and Scott's for his suits. One down the Arcade. Burton's. Then, of course, the Co-op was a big store in the town - you could buy almost anything.

The Co-op also had a Food Department there and they had the overhead cash system which you put your money in after you had made your purchases over the counter. They cut your cheese, sliced your bacon to how thick you wanted it, bashed the butter into shape with wooden bats, and dry goods they weighed up for you and packed them in little blue bags. You were also able to sit down on a chair while you were waiting or ordering.

I used to go to Moss's, the grocers, with mother; sat on the armchairs - all the smells. I remember also the lady coming round to take the order - Mrs. Saunders. I can picture her now. She had a full length, great big thick heavy leather coat on. She would come round to take my mother's order. I guess it was because she was having babies and things. It would be delivered a couple of days later. It was in Leys Avenue and a few doors up was Moss's Health Food Shop which go back a long time I think.

Moss's was a wonderful food shop. It smelled of ground coffee and ham 'off the bone'. I remember sitting on a tall, spindly chair because I couldn't reach the marble topped counter.

I remember quite a few of the shops. The Co-op and Nott's the bakers were in Eastcheap, near Munt's the toy shop. Then came the butcher's and Cheetham's the greengrocers, run by two sisters and perhaps a brother as well, much earlier.
The butchers we called "Porky Broughtons". It was full of hanging meat, birds and rabbits with sawdust all over the floor. Porky Broughton as his nickname suggests was very round, with a friendly face, full of double chins, He was always dressed immaculately in a straw boater, bow tie and striped apron. I remember drawing him when I got home one day.
Down Leys Avenue we had Woolworth's, a Health Food Store with, if I remember correctly, interesting tiles on the wall. I do remember the smell of fragrant herbs, vegetarian fruit bars, dried fruit and even dried bananas - a special treat as, with the war on, transporting bananas and

WH Smith staff 1952

oranges was very difficult. This shop was a paradise for gourmets who loved variety in their diets, and an antidote to rationing.

Further down Leys Avenue, before the Arcade, we had a haberdashery shop, the Co-op had it later but it might have been Nicholls before, or maybe Nicholls was further down. This shop had a fascinating system of canisters, pulleys and string, when you paid for your goods, the money would travel off, on the system and the change and receipt returned.

Going further down Leys Avenue, before the Wynd, we had Woolworth's, then even further down Spinks the drapers. Memory gets hazy after this but I do remember the long counters of Woolworth's and the wooden floorboards.

Before the shopping precinct, there was a blacksmith in Commerce Lane. Whitehead's taxi service was in Commerce Avenue at the back of the Broadway Cinema. There were houses and garages and the little old Church Rooms. There was a little hall there - I've forgotten the name now - but we played a county table tennis match there once. That was the only time I remember going into it. We used to walk the path round it to get from the old Nott's Bakers round through where is now the entrance to the supermarket, and just walk up there into Commerce Avenue. The blacksmith used to live near the traffic lights on Baldock Road - the end house. I remember seeing horses being shod there. I used to go and have a look.

There were stables on the road leading off from the Wynd. You used to go down behind Dean's furniture shop. There were a set of stables there (it now belongs to Howes and Boughton). The stables were there for dairy horses. I used to go along there and earn half-a-crown a week just for cleaning them out. I used to like that.

I can remember going to the Pioneer Laundry, now James Hayes. They used to do a bag wash service. You took it in the morning and collected it at night. Living in Broughton Hill I used to go sometimes and collect it for my mum, and they would do ironing and that sort of thing for you as well. The man from Moss's used to come round and take the order. Moss's was very nice to go into. You knew everybody personally there, and the smell of coffee beans in there was really lovely. I can remember Nott's the baker coming round. He used to come about Tuesday, Thursday and Saturday, I think, to us in Broughton Hill. He used to sell bars of chocolate as well. I always liked dark chocolate and I used to get Cadbury's dark bars.

I remember going to the Magnet at the top of Leys Avenue. Mr Rogers was there, and he used to have a quarter pound box of Dairy Box for my mum, and 20 or 40 Capstan full strength for my dad. I also remember one of my jobs was on Saturday morning, when I used to go up to the County Cycle Stores and get the accumulator for the radio. We used to have two accumulators. By about Friday the reception was getting quite bad so I was always pleased to be up there prompt on Saturday morning and get the new accumulator from Mr Wright at the County Cycle Stores. They were heavy. They were like a glass battery with a carrying handle. Also there used to be those huge batteries. I know I used to delight in taking them to bits, and inside there were all small ones, sort of lead plates.

Before my wife came back to number eight in 1942 the grocer used to deliver his stuff from a horse and cart. If Granny was not in, he would let himself in, go through the shelves in the kitchen and leave the things he could see that she needed on the kitchen table and settle up when he saw her later. Hartley, the seed merchant, also made their rounds with a horse and cart selling, amongst other things, paraffin by the pint from a fifty-gallon drum. In those days many houses used paraffin burners to heat the bedrooms that had no fireplace.

I can remember Mr Field with his horse and his two churns of milk on the back. He used to come down the garden and come to the house and mum used to put her jug out and he would say "Do you want a pint or a half pint?" He had these stainless steel measures and he put it straight into your jug. I think that carried on during part of the war. There was also Mason and Cason, another milkman from Station Road, where the betting shop is now. There was a dairy at the back there. Billy Field, he had his horses in Commerce Avenue. There was a blacksmith up there. There was Mr Topham who had a monkey in his garage. It used to throw spanners around. He had a highly polished Austin, which used to stand out when it came out into Leys Avenue.

I can remember having my first push bike from Munt's in Eastcheap. There was also Cheetham's, a greengrocer in Eastcheap. The two Cheetham brothers always used to wear straw hats, which was quite unique. Close by there was a pork butcher, a really large man that used to tower over me. I used to go in there and get pigs' trotters and things like that. Fishy Furr down the Wynd - we used to go down there and get our fish. They used to come round as well, as did Hartley's. My mum used to get candles and paraffin, etc.

I remember Woolworth's in Leys Avenue, with its wooden floors and tins of biscuits. Grocers shops had marble counters and weighed things in front of you and put them in blue paper bags. There was Russell's the chemist in Leys Avenue. I remember going in there with my sister to be weighed. I suppose the National Health Service was just coming in. My sister was weighed in a thing like a basket, but I had to stand. We were weighed and measured - I suppose to check on our growth.

Leys Avenue, 1949

In January 1911, Mr E.E. Russell started up his own business as a chemist in Station Road, Letchworth and lived over the premises for many years. There were approximately 150 employees who worked for Russell's in the area. At the Station Road shop I worked with about 15 people. Mr Russell was a good employer and fair with his staff. As well as being a pharmacist he was also an optician.

The company had been well established when I started working there in August 1942. Mr Russell had written to my school (St Mary's School at Stotfold) asking if any school leavers would be interested in a job at the Letchworth shop. There were only two of us at the time that were leaving school. I attended an interview and was then offered the job. I started at Russell's on the following Monday after finishing at school. I was 14 years old.

I started there as a junior working in the manufacturing and packing department which included the washing of the containers and measures. In those days we had to label all the bottles and jars individually and then cover them with cellophane. It was a varied and interesting job, making and packing all the old fashioned remedies such as zinc and castor oil cream and senna pods and many more items. I worked in the packing department for two to three years before moving into what we called the 'Drug Room'. This was actually dealing with the preparations of the drugs for the shop's prescriptions.

On a daily basis we had deliveries from various firms. The person that sticks in my mind the most was the 'railway man', Alec Everett. He would arrive with his horse and cart delivering small parcels. He was a very jovial man who had a lot of sayings. I remember that Alec came from Royston.

In the late 1950s, the manufacturing and packing department moved to Baldock, to the Maltings on the corner of Whitehorse Street and Clothall Road. By this time there were seventeen Russell shops in the area. Over the years, the name of the company on the manufacturing side changed to Rusco Ltd, however the shops still remained as Russell's Chemist.

Every year a party for the staff was organised in the Icknield Halls. Each employee who had worked for the firm for 21 years was presented with a watch. In 1960, after working there for nearly 20 years, I left to have a baby. However I was still lucky enough to receive my watch for 21 years service. In those years, I learnt a lot about the pharmacy industry thanks to Mr Russell.

My father, E.H. Howes, opened his dispensing opticians at the Colonnade in 1935. He sold the business in 1961. He joined the A.R.P. during the War. He met Indians at work who needed spectacles and they were invited to our Station Road home. I remember they were polite and always stood up when my mother entered the room. We had photographs with them taken by the Misses Clutterbuck in Icknield Way. You could not get film during the War so you had to go to a photographer. The Indians called my father Doctor as he wore a short white jacket at work.

We would walk almost everywhere in those days. There were two little corner shops local to us, on the corner of Bedford Road and Bursland. They were called Waller's and the Ottaway Stores. This saved a lot of shoe leather, as the town was so much further. The horses and carts eventually stopped delivering milk, cars and vans were much more common. Just the odd rag and bone cart or visiting scrap metal carts.

I used to love going to the little shops on the corner. It seemed like Aladdin's cave, full of smells and interesting shapes and colours. Eventually I was old enough to go to Mrs Waller's or Ottaway's on my own, or with my sister. I do remember a Mr Waller earlier, but not the latter years. I expect he died and Mrs Waller carried on, on her own. Both shops sold sweets and necessary items. I remember Mrs Waller had big bags of sugar in front of the counter. She would scoop out the sugar onto a weighing machine, and then transfer it to blue sugar bags, or if she had run out, a carefully folded cone of paper. Twice a week we walked to the town, I think it was Tuesday and Thursdays when we were off school. For us, Letchworth library was a very important part of the visit. The children's library was on the left, opposite the Broadway Cinema, and I don't think we were allowed in the grown up library in those days. We had to cross the Arena to get to the library; this was a big open space in the middle of the town.

Where the precinct is now, going in from Leys Avenue was a bakery (Nott's) and Whitehead's garage and then a row of terraced cottages. On the other side was Minnie Brown's the hairdresser, and the Co-op bakery. One or two things have stayed the same however; I still go to the Optician at the corner of Eastcheap and Leys Avenue that I did in 1945, and the florists next door was once Marshall's whom everyone knew.

The variety of shops in the fifties was vast; and the choice of small cafes also. There was Ruth's Pantry in Leys Avenue with its check tablecloths and high tea; Wallace's at the top of Station Road which belonged to the dairy and sold the most delicious coffee made with coffee essence (like Camp) and all milk. The People's Hall was a huge place, something like a Lyons Corner House; and the Co-op tea rooms in Eastcheap within the shop was very popular, and always busy.

The Herts Pictorial had an office in the Arcade. I remember that because when I was a kid I used to deliver to a couple of firms in the Arcade. I think there was a greengrocer called Richardson. Further down there was a chemist called Hooper's, and another shop in Leys Avenue was Underwood's, a general dealer. In those days they always used to wear brown smocks, in that sort of trade.

In Station Road it was a sort of village atmosphere almost, because the shops there did not change. We had next door but one to us on one side Mrs Simmonds selling cakes, groceries, sweets, tobacco etc, and on the other side the well-known hardware shop of Mr Llewellyn and a bit further down Russell's the chemist. There was a butcher's shop on the corner of the Wynd, and then on the other corner there was a dairy. Then a bit further down was Bollen's newsagent. With the improvement of the houses on the opposite side of Station Road the shops seemed to do well, and they seemed to stay in the same hands for many years. It is still a rarity to see a closed and empty shop in Station Road; they seem to survive pretty well. Also Cliff Wright had a cycle store, which later became a television and radio shop, on the corner of the Arcade. On the other corner was Bennett's the jewellers, which I think was one of the early Letchworth shops, along with his brother's garage across the road.

I can remember Munt's, Underwood's, Cheetham's in Eastcheap, a very grumpy Mr. Percy Beddoe at the sweet shop. He used to frighten me to death. We always went in there to get sweets but he was so grumpy. Then there was Stoke's down on the bottom corner. Two little ladies would serve you with sweets and ice cream. You used to have bulls eyes there, a tuppenny cone - Lyons Ice-Cream.

Food! How I loved every mouthful and still do.
Findlay's for salted peanuts and penny chews, the Wynd for fish and

chips served in grease-proof paper and wrapped in newspaper; Nott's for vanilla ice-cream and chocolate sauce - the best in the world: I've tried all other versions; and the Cabin for Smith's Crisps with the - often damp - salt in the dark blue paper twist. Oh, and Crunchie Bars, Five Boys, Cadbury's Milk Tray and a hundred other fatty, sugary delights.

A child still, I treat myself to a tour round the town. Oh for one of Mr Wegmuller's home-made ice creams in the Arcade! Here's Cheerful Charlie, the station porter who sometimes forgot to put in his teeth. Over there the whitewashed cottage of Daisy Perrot a wizened 'witch' who gave me maths tuition and had written 'Teach Yourself Swahili'. Hello Josie, who cut the ham at the International Stores and gave me a slice to taste. Good morning Mr Humm who set me astride his horse in the Wynd. Blow me down, it's Della, the gloriously hard boiled blonde who reigned over Nott's cafe's cash till, proudly displaying the mink earrings she had ordered through a woman's magazine. And sorry, poor Derek in Foster and Scott's the outfitters, for having to bear the brunt of my tirade about not being allowed to buy that strawberry coloured mohair sweater. (But I was only doing it as an early form of men's liberation: why should schoolboys have to wear only grey, navy or forest green?)

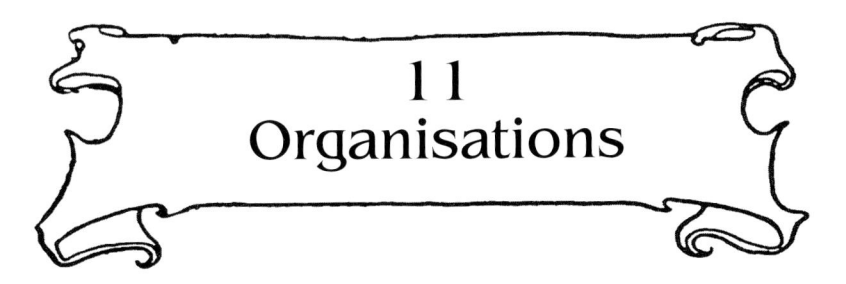

11 Organisations

During and after the War Letchworth had many organisations for both young people and adults.

Girl Guides

I was in the Girl Guides for a long time. That had an attachment with St. Thomas à Beckett. I was in the Brownies first and then I was a Girl Guide. I did try my hand at first aid but I didn't seem to get on too well with that. I mean I got married very young - I was only 17-and-a-half when I got married in 1954.

Through the Guides I helped out at the Forces Canteen which was in the Church Rooms, which have long gone now - but they were in Commerce Avenue. We used to go there and make tea and do what we could with the very small amount of rationing that was available for things like that.

Youth Club

I used to go to Letchworth Youth Club. I was playing table tennis down there in the 1950s; I was twenty. We had an evening table tennis club in Howard Hall.

I remember the Youth Club at Howard Hall. My mother called it the girls' club, because it had been a girls' club when she was young. I was still at the Grammar School, so it was probably about the late 1950s. There was a dance hall above the Co-op. We used to go to dances there as well. There were halls opposite, over Nott's. There were a lot more public dances then. As a child if we went out on a Saturday shopping we used to go for a coffee at the People's House, at the top of Station Road. They had murals round the wall. I found that fascinating. I remember going into Nott's down Leys Avenue for morning coffee and that. Boots was opposite, and they had a lending library at the back. There was a MacFisheries, selling wet fish. I remember Fine Fare in Eastcheap. My grandfather worked in there for a while. I got a weekend job there when it opened. I was at the College then. It was a bit of extra money, stacking the shelves. On a Friday night they were open until eight o'clock. That was quite revolutionary. I used to do five to eight on Friday night, then Saturdays.

Girls' Training Corps

Like all those who grew up during the Second World War, my teenage years were coloured and shaped by wartime conditions. When I left school I joined the GTC (Girls' Training Corps), a pre-service organisation equivalent to the ATC and the Army and Sea Cadets. We met two or three times a week at Norton Road School for drill and classes in various subjects - one was aircraft recognition, I remember. We did not have a complete uniform but wore our own navy skirts and white blouses with a navy blue tie - the navy forage cap and badge were the only regulation items though the officers had a full uniform.

In the Letchworth Company we had a special link with the ATC, as our commandant, Mrs G Critchley, was the wife of the commander of the local squadron and we were drilled by Warrant Officer Walker of the ATC. The town had a lot of public parades during those years, to launch special savings drives, for instance, and we took part in many civic events. We were delighted when a report in one of the local papers described us as "marching like young guardsmen"! I remember that on one occasion on Norton Common we found it very difficult to keep in step on grass - especially when the Army Cadets' brass band was in conflict with the drum and fife band of the ATC! The GTC provided us with social life too. We had small regular dances at St. George's Hall, and bigger events at the Icknield Halls and the Co-op Hall in Letchworth.

ORGANISATIONS 121

Above: No 303 (Letchworth) Company Girls' Training Corps (GTC) Women's Rally, May 1943

Below: Girls' Training Corps Dance, Icknield Hall, Letchworth, February 1943

I joined the Girls' Life Brigade at the Free Church with my three cousins. The uniform was navy and red. I also had been to Sunday School. We used to make woollen balls, suitable for baby carriages.

WVS

When we were very young we decided we ought to join up and do something. This was just at the beginning of the War. So I joined the WVS and helped at the Canteen set up at the Cloisters for soldiers on the searchlight at Willian. By a strange coincidence, many years later we broke down in our car in Scotland and the AA man who helped us was one of those soldiers who had been on that searchlight at Willian.

Further on in my teens I joined the Women's Voluntary Services and worked in the canteen in Commerce Avenue (the old church rooms), during which time I met many service men and women, many of whom came to train at the Government Training Centre in Pixmore Way.

Round Table

A lot of the young men I knew joined Round Table. They were keen to get together, they had a lot in common: they had all been in the Forces in some respect. So a lot of fun was had with very little money and a lot of work was done for the town. They built a Paddling Pool for the Briar Patch children and had an annual fair to raise money for all sorts of things. I remember the very first one was for a flood disaster in Canada - in Winnipeg - and they raised £100 and that seemed at that time like a great deal of money. That would have been in the late forties.

Round Table building the paddling pool at Briar Patch Children's Home

ORGANISATIONS 123

Above: Round Table rally

Below: Medieval Banquet celebrating Round Table's 21st anniversary.

The Salvation Army

I played in the Band over a span of years. I have played more than one instrument. I started off my career playing a baritone moving on to a tenor horn; I have played a tuba.

I am speaking about my connection with Letchworth branch of the Salvation Army because I have been associated with this movement all my life. Now in 1939, with the outbreak of war, I remember well it starting on a Sunday when we managed to hold our services as normal except at six o'clock when we should have had a meeting in the street. This was cancelled because King George VI was broadcasting to the nation regarding the Prime Minister, Mr Neville Chamberlain's earlier declaration of war. Soon after that, actually that weekend, the evacuees were arriving from London. We had two buildings, and still have, in Norton Way North, beside our main citadel we had, what was known as the 'hut' where the Sunday School was held, among other youth events. This was given for the three years of the War for a rest centre and drop-in centre where they could come every day of the week. There were armchairs brought in and meals laid on and this sort of thing, so we helped to make the evacuees' life a little more bearable as they were away from home, mainly from London.

After the blitz finished, in the middle of 1941, a lot drifted back to London, so the rest centre was then given up and we were able to resume our normal activities. In the Salvation Army, as is well known, we have a band that conducts meetings in the streets in different parts of the town every Sunday. The 1943 band included a number of young people who were helping the senior band because a lot of our people were away in the forces.

The Salvation Army Band 1941

We now move on to the years following the Second World War and our Salvation Army. Our men came back from the forces and our band improved in numbers. But of course the band is not the only section of the Corps that we have. We have a thriving young people's work. I have a photograph of the junior choir, called C Company, in 1954 with its leader Mrs Muriel Heritage and myself sitting at the piano. Also at that time we had a thriving Cub pack under the leadership of Miss Hannah Shannon. Throughout many years the Salvation Army work carried on locally and internationally. Every Christmas Day the Salvation Army band plays carols at the local Hospice. This particular time it was the old Chalkdell Hospital in Hitchin, what is now the Lawrence Ward. I have a photograph of the band standing outside with a number of the nurses who were on duty that morning as we played carols at that time. Moving on to 1956, it was the year of the Hungarian uprising, and we remember that a number of these refugees came from Hungary and they were also centred at the Hostel, the old Ascot building, the Hostel behind it in Pixmore Avenue. On a couple of occasions our band went to conduct concerts, and one was Christmas 1956, the revolution taking place in October, and we went that Christmas and we were well received by the Hungarian refugees. Of course, some time after that many of them returned to Europe or found homes and positions in this country, so they were no longer at our Hostel.

Being one of a family of Church members - The Salvation Army - I remember every Sunday night at the open-air service. They had a band and met every Sunday night in the Colonnade in Station Place. There was something happening in the town every week.

Salvation Army at Chalkdell Hospital, Christmas 1954

My father - when he came to Letchworth - he was already a keen member of the Brass Band in Suffolk - so the attraction of the Brass Band of the Salvation Army had an appeal to him. So that was the influence of the Salvation Army all those years ago - and we still attend.

St John Ambulance

I was a member of the St John Ambulance Brigade in the late fifties. I was made up to sergeant, and I was in charge of their ambulance. I was the sergeant in charge of the ambulance that actually bought their new ambulance. It was a Standard Atlas van, which we bought through Thompsons Garage at Hitchin. This was modified for us by Green and Nickels so it could take a stretcher. It had ramps for wheelchairs, but not for a stretcher, so Green and Nickels had to modify it for us.

I was in charge of that for many many years. One of the duties I had was to take it up to London with a number of members to Winston Churchill's funeral. I was on duty at Seymour House, and I had the privilege (or pleasure!) of stopping the band of the Horse Guards because I was blocking the way, so they had to stand there marking time until I came to move the ambulance. We had to be up there at seven in the morning. We also went on parade at one point in Hyde Park where we were presented to the Queen. She came round in a Land Rover. I can remember a Mrs Elliott, who was a great friend of mine, as we were walking up to the ambulance station to get the ambulance, saying "Where are you going today?" I said, "Oh, we are going to see the Queen" and she said, "Oh yes, to see the Queen" and burst out laughing. I don't think she believed us, but we did go to see the Queen. We went to Hyde Park, and we had a lovely day there.

I was in the St. John Ambulance Brigade until the middle sixties. I carried on until my father was taken ill, then I found I was more and more involved with the shop. I didn't have the time to carry on with St. John.

People I remember: Bill Savage, of the St. John Ambulance Brigade, was a great character. I think everyone in Letchworth knew him. He had only one eye. The other was a glass eye. He was stone deaf. He used to run around on this little motorised scooter. When I was in St. John earlier on he was the Superintendent. At that time, he could be sitting at one end of the table with his back to you, but you could never walk up on him. You could never catch him out. He always had a sense of somebody being there, although he could not hear a thing. He used to lip read. I remember we had the Hertfordshire Show at Willian, and I was on duty with him. He got a bit of grit in his glass eye, and he took it out and cleaned it and put it back in and said to me "Is it straight?" He lived in Spring Road with his first wife. Unfortunately she died then he remarried and carried on his St. John duties well into he seventies. He was a great old boy, loved by many people.

Top: The Sunbeams with Leader Rhoda Bates, 1957

Centre: The Singing Company in 1954

Bottom: Letchworth Salvation Army Cub Pack in 1954

12
Televison comes to Letchworth

Television came to Letchworth in the late 1940s, although a few sets were available before the War. It was a luxury when it was first introduced, but slowly more and more people bought a set.

One of the things I remember in particular was my parents getting a television set in time for the Royal Wedding in November 1947. It was a nine-inch screen Philips combined radio and television and we got it from Ken Crump in Baldock. Because we were one of the few people in our area with a television set, when there were occasions like the Royal Wedding, cup finals, boat races, or anything else we'd have a room full of people. It was a real social occasion. I can remember the Cup Final in 1948 between Blackpool and

Manchester United and several of my father's work mates came up to look at this match. At the end of it I cried my eyes out because Blackpool had lost four - two to Manchester United. One of my dad's friends gave me half-a-crown and that was a lot of money at that time, so I felt it was worth it.

The TV at that time wasn't on continuously from early morning to late at night. There were breaks. Very often they had serial stories going on - films and things like that. I can remember in particular one cowboy story that went on for about five days and another one involving aircraft and there would be perhaps eight, nine, ten of us all sitting glued to the television.

As time went on, more and more people got televisions and there was less and less socialising. I think the last time we had a big social occasion around the television was for the Coronation in 1953. That was a very wet day and I can remember watching the Coronation on the television in the morning and then going down to the Common in the evening for the fireworks display which was a bit of a damp squib because of the weather.

As to television, there was one in Orchard Road before the War that was a local wonder. Gradually the ownership increased and thereby the loss of our choice of cinemas.

The Television Exhibition held at the People's Hall

My great uncle lived at St Ippolyts, and he was the only one in the family who had a television, so the whole family went to watch the Coronation on his television. It was black and white, with a magnifying thing over the screen to make it bigger. The screen was about nine inches, but it was a big cabinet type of thing that stood on the floor.

Then one day the neighbours invited us to see the boat race between Oxford and Cambridge. I thought we were actually going, but it turned out to be on their newly acquired television, a box in the corner! Soon after we invested in a television.

Before the War, Stanley Lee had a radio shop down in Hitchin. He was somebody who one could almost call a pioneer in television, like Clifford Wright. It was not until the early fifties that people in general became interested in having a television set, and that was when Wright's shop started to sell them and they became popular.

The main store selling television sets was County Cycle Stores, which, as its name suggests, had sold bicycles. The increasing popularity of television meant the store eventually stopped selling cycles and changed its name to CV Wright & Sons.

Initially the business was cycles mainly, then radio, then television came in just before the War. I can remember a television, which was an old one, in my bedroom during the War, covered with a blanket. My father had a television in 1936, when it actually opened.

I came to work in my father's shop. Initially it was called the County Cycle Stores. My father bought it in, I think, 1936 from George Munt who also owned Munt's Cycles in Eastcheap. My father bought it from him. It was then called the County Cycle Stores, and my father's name was Clifford Wright, who was actually the brother of Philip Wright who was organist and choirmaster of the Free Church for about thirty or forty years. He was also choirmaster for the Arcadians for twenty-five or thirty years.

Round about the 1950s, televisions cost about 78 guineas. They ranged from about 78 or 80 guineas. Everything was in guineas then. That was a lot of money when you consider the average wage was about five pounds a week. All you got was BBC, and it was black and white, and that was it. A little twelve-inch screen.

We decided to put on some publicity. There had always been an exhibition in London at Earls Court or Olympia for many years, about all the new models as televisions came out. At that time a lot of people could not get up to London, so we decided to have our own exhibition in Letchworth. The first one we had was in the first half of the fifties. We held it in the People's House and we got stands from the main makers that we dealt with - Pye, Philco, Pilot, etc., and also electrical goods such as Ever Ready and Electrolux. We held the exhibition at the People's Hall, which is in Station Road. The first one was opened by Ernest Gardiner, the Chairman of the Council. The following year we did the same sort of thing and we managed to get Arthur Askey, the well-known comedian from the radio, to come down. I managed to get a day off school, and he came in and saw me and he said, "What are you doing here?" I said, "I got a day off school so that I could see you", and he said, "I suppose I am as good enough excuse as anybody to have a day off school", and he opened the exhibition for us that day. The following year we had a third exhibition - the last one that we had - and that was opened by Seaman and Farrell of Forsyth, Seaman and Farrell, very well known radio comedians.

Our store not only sold televisions and cycles. We also did a lot of other electrical stuff, all sorts of things. We did charging up batteries. The old radios had an accumulator. We used to charge them up twice a week. We charged I think a penny or two pence a charge. People would come in and drop one off on one day and pick another fully charged one up; then bring that back two or three days later and pick up the second one. We used to sell sports gear as well - tennis racquets and that sort of thing. We used to string tennis racquets in the shop - I have re-strung many.

Staff of County Cycle Stores with Arthur Askey (3rd from left)

People viewing the TVs at the exhibition

I did not do any courses as such in those days. I just went in there as a shop assistant. I was behind the counter serving in the shop, and doing electrical things. I learned from the people in the shop - Jim Beard, and Bob Adams who were doing the cycles. Then some years later our television engineer left us and we had one chap inside, and they sent me out to pick up the televisions and bring them in. I kind of had a crash course then, and said, "Why do you bring this one in when all it needed was a valve?" I learned it virtually by practical experience. It was not until later years that I actually went to college and did a radio and television servicing course.

In the early part the business was cycles. It was called the County Cycle Stores. In the later fifties the cycles were getting larger and becoming mopeds (motorised bicycles), and televisions were coming in and they were getting more and more. The two were expanding, so one of them had to go. My father decided to give up the cycles and concentrate on just televisions. As we were selling just televisions then and not cycles we had to change the name. We could not call ourselves County Cycle Stores, if we did not sell bicycles. So we changed in 1958 or 59 to C V Wright and Son.

We did as lot of public address work, not only in Letchworth. We did Norton May Day every year until that finished, and all over the North London area, Hertingford and Enfield, horse shows and gymkhanas, we did the loud speakers for them. In the Icknield Halls in Ralph Nott's time local organisations used to have their dinner dances there. We used to sit up in the balcony with the equipment. We had the contract, as it were, with Ralph Nott. He did not want the bother of doing the loud speakers, so we permanently installed speakers in the two halls, with a switchboard up on the balcony. Whenever there was a dinner dance - which was most Wednesdays, Fridays and Saturdays in the winter months - we would go up there and fix up microphones in the bars to relay the speeches at the dinners, then transfer after the dinner was finished to the Master of Ceremonies for the dance afterwards. During the winter there were on average probably about three nights a week. Then during the summer it eased off. There were all sorts of dinners - factory dinners, Round Table dinners, Rotary dinners, Masonic dinners, Chamber of Trade dinners. We had many celebrities there - the Mud Larks, Bernard Monchin and his Rio Tango Band - a great character he was. Wilson Hill had one of the local bands - a very nice bloke. Claude Charles - he was another one, and Peter Haydon. They had the Radio and Television Retailers' Association dinner there, and there were usually two or three celebrities at the dinners as well. The Television Viewers' Association was an organisation that carried on in the fifties but gradually petered out in the sixties.

In our house we had a television set in the lounge. We used to clear the lounge out when it was Cup Final day, and we would put chairs

County Cycle Stores' public address system

in there and a lot of our friends would come round and sit in the lounge and watch the Cup Final. My mother used to bring cups of tea in at half time. For the Coronation I can remember we put televisions in the Free Church Hall, the Central Methodist Hall and the old St. George's Hall. We had them working so that members of the public could go there and see the Coronation for themselves, because a lot of people in those days did not have television. So we did three halls, and I can remember going round in the van checking to make sure the televisions still kept working. They were not as reliable then as they are now.

In those days, if any television was not working properly it was possible to thump it with your fist and very often it would reactivate itself.

That was because in those days they used to have valves, and the pins were very thin. Being after the War, there was a glut of valves called Mier 50 which had very thin pins. They used to tarnish and we used to have to go round every so often and clean them. If the set packed up you would give it a thump and that was enough just to move the valves and make contact again, so the set would keep working.

There were other places like Foster & Scott where we would put in a television. When there was the Boat Race or the Cup Final, and between serving customers - although on special sports days there were not a lot of customers about - staff used to congregate out the back watching whatever the sport was. They weren't really being very happy if somebody came in and wanted to buy something!

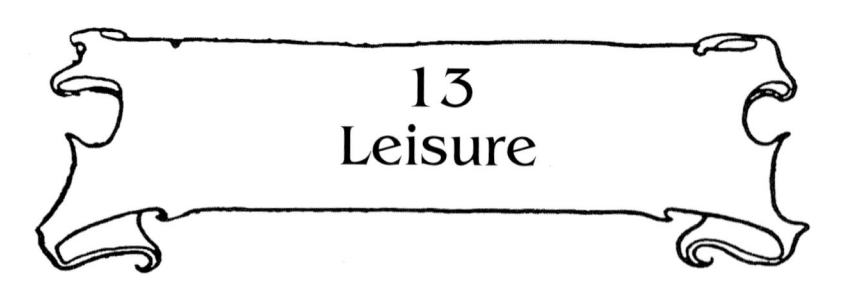

13 Leisure

Leisure activities in Letchworth both during and after the War tended to revolve mainly around the cinemas and the dances halls.

Cinema

Letchworth had two cinemas - the Broadway and the Palace. The latter was commonly referred to as the "Flea Pit".

I remember the cinema, the flea-pit which was the Palace. We went into the ninepennies. If you were well off you went into the one shilling and sixpennies. We had two cinemas to chose from in those days - the Palace and the Broadway.

People actually used to queue up in those days. They would stand for an hour or more in those days. At the Broadway it would go round the corner and down Gernon Road, down to where we used to leave our cycles.

In those days we used to queue for the pictures at the Broadway and the queue would often go right round in the bit where the cleaning shop is now, right round the back of the Broadway. Going to the pictures was a regular hobby in those days. There were two cinemas then, the Broadway and the Palace. Some of the kids used to go and open the exit door, if they could, and let their friends in. The Fire Station was next door.

The Palace - the flea-pit! In the four pennies on a Saturday morning. Brilliant! Bag of bullseyes and that was a treat. If you'd got sixpence you were made! That was your pocket money if you'd worked hard enough you might have got sixpence.

When we were children, or even teenagers, we had a double-bill. There was always a 'B' film you could watch, with an ice-cream in the middle. We had the Pathe News at the Palace, I remember, and the Gaumont News at the Broadway. The Palace was always scruffy, hence it was known as the 'Flea Pit'.

The old Palace Cinema had partitions at the back, with curtains. Every time the film started the curtain used to draw. You never knew what was going on in there. You could shut the cubicles up so that you could not see the screen. I was too young then, but all the fellows with their girls drew the curtains as soon as the picture started and away they went. In the end the management got wise to it and dismantled all those and took them out. That was a laugh, that was.

Most of my leisure time really was spent in the Broadway and Palace cinemas, before television. I mean, what with the films being changed on Wednesday, we had a choice of four times a week, and later it came to Sunday as well. Most of my time was really spent at the pictures. Apart from occasional concerts at St Francis' Theatre, (often featuring comedians who were rather risqué for the time), Eastcheap was the entertainment centre.

Sport

Sport featured prominently in Letchworth life as well, with tennis, hockey, football and cricket all popular.

During this time I was involved in sports - tennis in particular at Letchworth Hall Tennis Club. I was Ladies' Captain for a time. It was very well known for its high standard. I think Letchworth was excellent for games. I played hockey in Letchworth, and Esther Brookes was the captain of the hockey team. I did not play for the

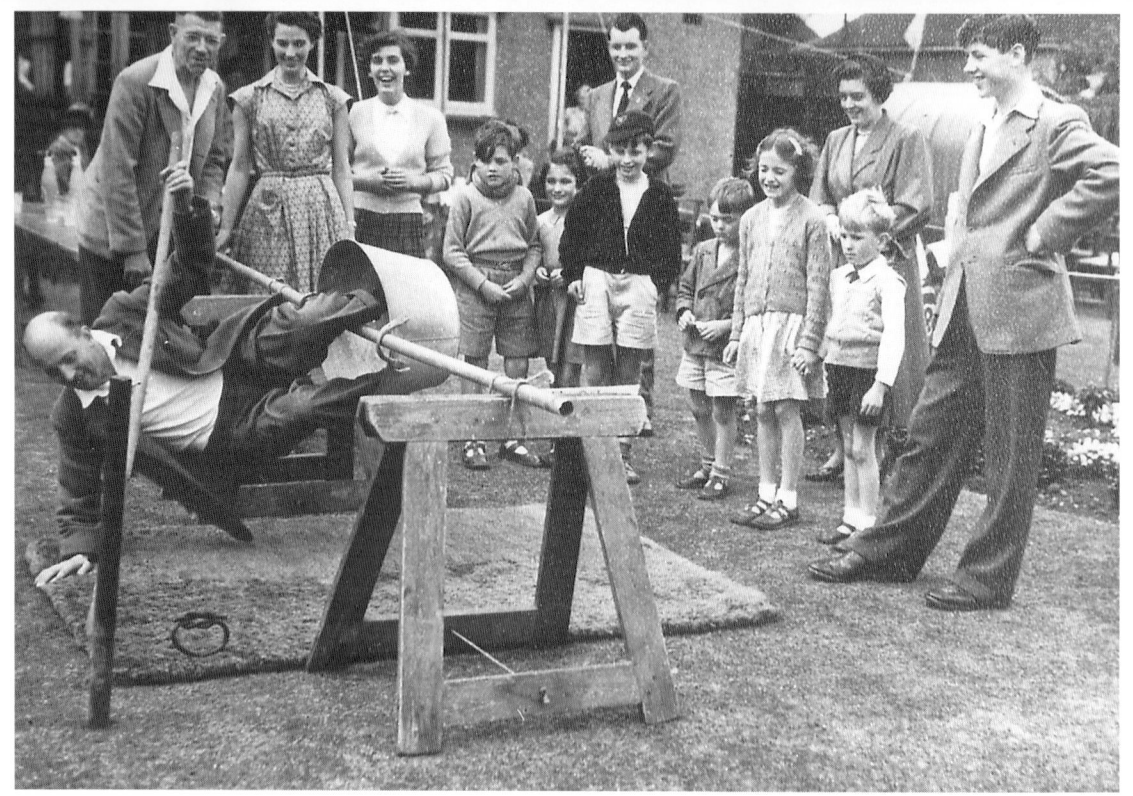

Above: Free Church Tennis Club Garden Party 1952

Above Right: Barn Dance

Below: St Michael's Folk Dance Group Party

Below Right: Letchworth Young Conservatives Dinner, held in the Icknield Halls early 1950s

LEISURE 137

You can't play Tennis with a Racket like this!

Have it repaired by experienced workmen on the premises
New season's gut now in stock
Repairs done in an hour
Restrings following day

County Cycle Stores
STATION ROAD, LETCHWORTH Tel. 297

Corinthians Cricket Club 1947

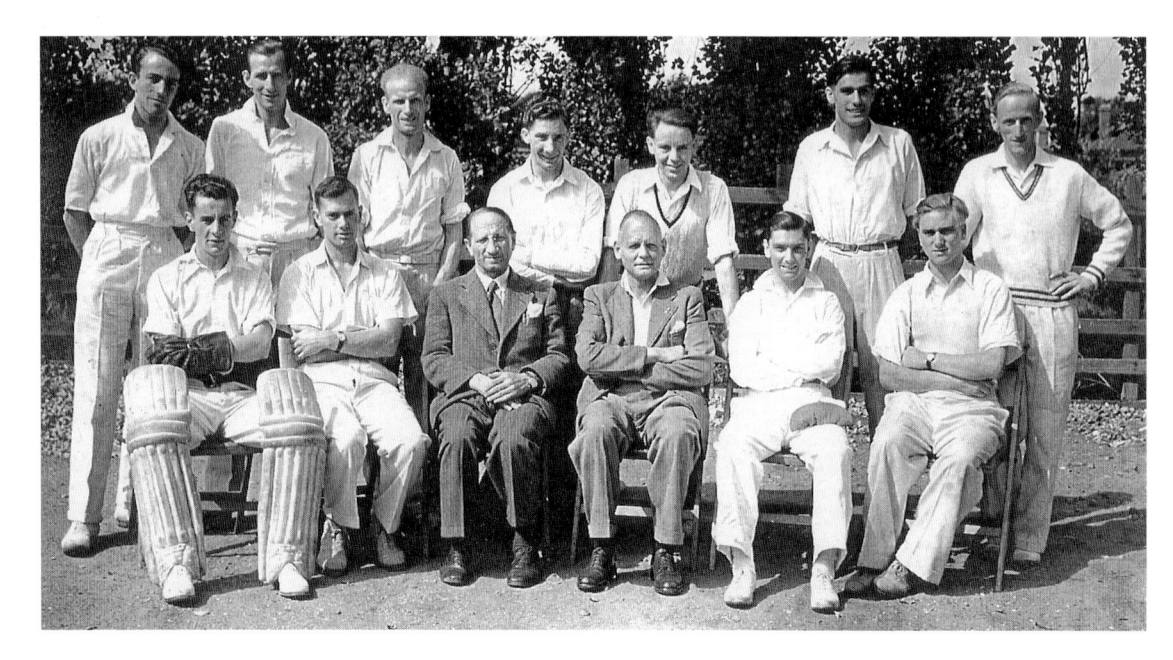

County, but I did play for Letchworth, and she was captain. She was a teacher at Westbury School and then she came out to Sandon as head mistress and she was a County Councillor. She did a lot of things. I played badminton, and there I came across Freda Diss. I knew quite a lot of people in Letchworth through working there, although I did not live there. I knew people through games.

Letchworth Corinthian Sports Club was formed just after the end of the war by returning servicemen recently demobilised. As the club had no ground, all matches, football and cricket were played away. Many clubs in the district and amongst the Cambridgeshire villages were pleased to accommodate this new team, which maintained a good club standard and acquitted itself well. It acquired a reasonable reputation which probably reached its zenith in the defeat of Letchworth at the Corner in the final of the Blackman Cup seven a side tournament.

We missed out on the 18 - 20 era, being away from home. We had lost what we had when we went in (the army). It was a difficult six months adjustment. I could not settle down for quite a while. I had a lot of interest in football. I played football at Letchworth and at Baldock, Royston and Stotfold. I played for town teams. As a schoolboy in 1949 in the short time I was at Norton Road School I was picked to play for Herts' schoolboys and played against Watford schoolboys and in some final of the Herts Schools Trophy. I only played one game but I ended up with a lovely solid silver medal. I played for Letchworth youth teams. I progressed to the reserves, on and off. Then finally I decided to go back to Newcastle, met a friend of mine I had known when I was up there and we started going out together again. I used to go up there every three weeks from Letchworth. Finally we got married in 1959, I think it was. Our first family was born in 1960.

Us sporting types used to spend a lot of time watching Letchworth Football Club in their Spartan League days. We also watched Letchworth Cricket Club on the corner in the summer. There were a few characters in Letchworth in those days - well known eccentrics.

I used to go to see Letchworth Football Club when I was young. Jackmans Place was at the end of the buildings really. At the end of Jackmans Place was all the fields over towards Baldock. The football ground was at the same place as it is now.

I have always followed Letchworth football. Old Bill Craft used to be outside the People's House on a Saturday night and we used to wait for the van to come from Luton to deliver what we called the "Green 'Un", which would give you all the news on all the local teams. I can remember in my early days I became the mascot of Letchworth and used to run out in front of the team, and I can remember three thousand plus being up there. Once we played a team from Portsmouth, I think it was, HMS Collingwood, and I had my picture on the front of the Herts Pictorial, with my costume on. It did deteriorate to when we used to say the faithful five hundred, but we never dreamt it would ever go below five hundred.

LETCHWORTH FOOTBALL CLUB'S SUCCESSFUL SEASON
President denies two rumours

Postwar Letchworth Football Club (Manager Jack Corney back row, right)

Letchworth Strollers in the 1950s

I used to love going up Letchworth Corner. I used to go up there to watch cricket, because it was such a nice setting up there, with the trees all round, and Letchworth Corner Post Office. St Christopher School was round the outside. They all used to walk in from St Christopher's to come and watch. One of Letchworth's best batsmen was Austin O'Neill, who was also a teacher at St.Christopher, so we often used to get the boys come and watch him.

If you wanted a glass of beer in those days you had to walk over the fields to Willian on a Sunday night. Lots of people used to do that, or go down to the Shoes at Norton. The Broadway was the first in Letchworth where you could go for a drink.

During the war when we had double summer time I can remember being up in Jackmans Place recreation ground, it must have been about a quarter to eleven at night and my mum coming up there to bring me home from playing football.

The Settlement

The Settlement was formerly the Skittles Inn – the "pub with no beer" – which had been built as a communal centre for families when the town was built. During and after the War dances and concerts were held there. Letchworth itself had no pubs, so residents had to go outside the town's boundaries for a drink.

I remember going to the Settlement. They used to have a concert or a dance for youngsters - once a month I believe. Then we used to go up to the Hermitage Halls - in Letchworth and in Hitchin. There were halls where Bott's, the insurance company, is now.

There were no pubs. We used to go to Hitchin. Hitchin station was the place for fights.

LEISURE 141

The Settlement

Top: The Ramblers' Group

Middle: The May Fair in 1958

Bottom: A Settlement Art Class in 1946

It was usually the Wilbury or the Shoes. My Dad used to use the Wilbury for years and years. We'd occasionally use the Chimneys. Harry Blane was the landlord there for years. We never had a pub in Letchworth, but Ebenezer Howard opened the first pub with no beer, the Settlement (the Skittles Inn). It's still there. Then as years went by, they brought the Broadway into Letchworth, the first pub with beer.

The Billiard Hall

The Billiard Hall in Leys Avenue seems to have been a place that many would wish to avoid!

The Billiard Hall in Leys Avenue was where all the bad boys ended up. It was above Burton's and was taken over by Fisher; he was a bookie and a nice guy. If the police in those days wanted someone, they'd go up to the billiard hall, just stand there and say "Just the man we want". No matter where you go you'd get a bad apple. My brother was up there in the billiard hall and he'd been drinking. The Gallards were taking advantage of him. He knocked Bill from the billiard hall upstairs, to right under the Arcade, right into Station Way. I saw him the next day and his face was twice the size. I was 13.

The Swimming Pool

Letchworth's outdoor swimming pool on the common was a popular place.

I remember the swimming pool opening. My father was a very good swimmer and he taught me to swim there when it first opened. I think it was just before the War that was built, about 1935.

I spent many happy days at the Letchworth outdoor swimming pool in the Common. That was very popular in my childhood. We used to get a season ticket.

During my last years at the Grammar School I was doing a lot of swimming in local competitions for Letchworth Swimming Club and we travelled by coach from venue to venue. Homework had to be done during the journey very often. Mrs Pooley was petitioning Letchworth Council for an indoor pool at that time, as in winter season we had to train in Marshall Street baths in London. I remember going to a council meeting when an indoor pool was on the agenda, supposedly to put forward our proposals or declare an interest, but we had to sit there all the time and not say a word.

The Co-op Fete

The Co-operative Stores in Eastcheap was a popular store, and their loyal customers were rewarded each year with a fete on the Arena.

One of my happy childhood memories in the 40's was the annual Co-op Fete that was on the Arena. This event was open to all the children of the parents who had a share in the Co-op.

I had two brothers and a sister. If your parents had a share number you were allowed to go to the fete every year. We would collect our tickets which were perforated into three parts. One was for the mat slide, the other part was for a sideshow. This was a machine with ping-pong balls popped up. If you caught one in a net you got a prize and then the third part of the ticket was for a little box which they gave us and it had two sandwiches, a cake and a drink in it. You had to sit in a certain roped-off area to eat it. In that area later on we had races and then it ended up with a fancy dress competition. So that was an annual event which we eagerly looked forward to. I think this was later taken over by the Round Table.

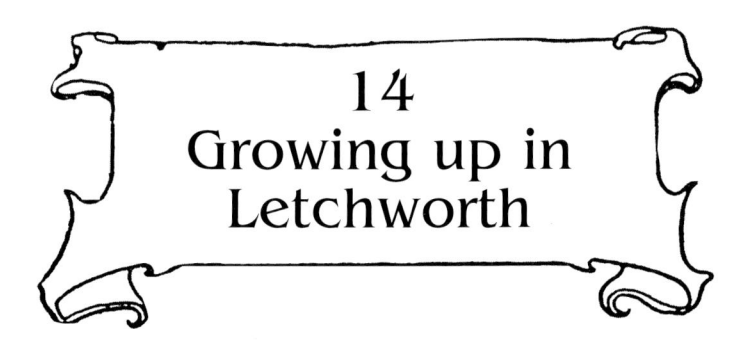

14
Growing up in Letchworth

Childhood in Letchworth is generally remembered as being good fun with a lot of freedom. The water that runs under the town and the River Pix on the Common seem to feature in a large number of the memories.

We had a marvellous time playing in the field opposite Wilbury School. There were prefabricated bungalows in Runnalow that backed onto it and we faced it. We had camps in the bushes and played endless games of rounders and cricket. Even in those days Bedford Road was busy and we were escorted across the road by an adult or older sibling. I remember when our neighbour, Mr Sturman, bought a car and we were all excited. He sometimes parked it in our drive because his house didn't have one.

We were quite near the railway and the cemetery and the pub. People used to walk up to the Two Chimneys because they could not drink in Letchworth. The Chimneys was outside the Letchworth boundary, in Bedfordshire then. It wasn't built up much. Romany Close was just fields. We used to play in the street. We used to go up to the Roman Camp, which was Wilbury. In summer we used to walk through the Common. We used to go as a group to go swimming. The swimming pool was not heated, either. We used to go from school. They used to have a board with the temperature written on, and we used to get there and it was 50 degrees, or 40 something.

Monklands was a quiet road until the evacuees came, and then it livened up. There were so many places to play without bothering other people. At the top of Monklands was a large pond in a meadow that later became Monks Close. We played for hours there, or at the Roman Camp opposite the Wilbury Hotel. The wooded area now designated a picnic area was reputed to be haunted and we went to gather blackberries and sloes there, always with an adult, for the bushes were high where all the best fruit was. There were two slopes in the Roman Camp where we used to take sleds when it snowed and had serious snowball fights. There were also two wide footpaths running parallel on either side of the small wood. One led to Cadwell Crossing where we walked seemingly forever to get to the river with our picnics. The other went as far as the Sparrowhawk wood into which we would walk until we reached a great fallen tree, and never daring to go further in. It was very thick in those days.

It is not commonly known that a great deal of water runs beneath Letchworth. From the bridge in Norton Way South there was once a deep ditch running along the front of the present garages there, which flowed with water, then continued underground as far as Norton where the ditches were once again in evidence in front of the private houses on the right hand side going down to the village. As children we used to jump them and cling on to the fence as a "dare". The pond at the top of Monklands came from an underground source naturally, as does the pond near Croft Lane where bulrushes grew.

Before the houses were built beside the church in Bedford Road there was a footpath leading down to the river Pix beside which was a derelict house and a fallen tree across the water. The lane went on to Wilbury Road. We used it as a short cut to school regardless of the tale of a murder there at the beginning of the century. A woman was supposed to have been strangled there.

I started horse-riding with a friend from Baldock Road, we went to Hitchin Riding Stables, which was situated opposite Grays Lane in Hitchin. The field we used was behind Wratten Road. Major Cunningham was very strict, but once he thought we were safe riding we used the bridleway to Oughton Head, behind the lavender fields

Mollie Langford School of Dancing 1949

and going towards Luton. We used to go potato picking and pea picking in groups, on the back of lorries with the Young Farmers to farms along the Hitchin/Luton border in order to increase our pocket money for the riding lessons.

Many of us girls went to ballet classes. There was Miss Childe-Warren or Molly Langford to choose between. I was cycled by my mother all over Letchworth to a variety of locations. The Cloisters, The Settlement and of course for the annual show, St Francis Theatre.

I remember when I was still at school, Sunday mornings Common View and Glebe Road were deadly enemies, and Sunday mornings we used to go down Icknield Way - all the factories and fields weren't there those days - and we used to play at roller skating. Two or three hours up and down the road: it was a beautiful surface. And it usually ended in a punch up, about dinnertime - the boys of Glebe Road versus Common View. Great fun, they were. There were some very good skaters among them.

Bikes and walking was the form of transport then. We used to go to Baldock quite a lot as a family. My mother, especially in the holidays, used to walk; go down the old Icknield Way, past the chalk pits at the bottom of Green Lane, down through what we used to call 'the roughy Baldock', which was a track like a bridle path to Baldock and which was a continuation of the old Icknield Way. There were a lot of big gypsy camps down there. Along Blackhorse Lane - there were always gypsies down there. We used to play a lot in those chalk pits as well. They weren't steep, but there were lots of bushes and things to play in. We had camps.

Jackmans Place rec. used to be the favourite place to play in those days. The park keeper used to come through to stop you cycling. Round the back of the houses there were laurel bushes down to the wire fence, and wasps used to nest in the ground. I can remember two or three times we used to get laurel branches and smack them as they came in and out. The worst case for me was I got stung just above the eye. I went running to my friend's Mum, Mrs Mynott. I daren't go home to my Mum because she would tell me off. Mrs Mynott put on vinegar or something. I went home and never told my Mum. In the morning, I couldn't open my eye, it was so swollen. I had to tell Mum then, so I got told off. When we had been hitting the wasps in the bushes Pauline got some in her hair and they stung her head, and she ran into the playing field part of the common there to get the wasps out. The silly things you do!

We used to walk over the fields from Jackmans Place to Willian Dell. There was a fox in there. We walked much more in those days. We played football in the street. We often had to go and ask for our ball back, and some people did not want to give it back, and made you wait. We used to roller skate down Pixmore Way to the town. It was a nice smooth road. I remember going to Roman Camp, and down the sandpit into the pine trees. When we used to cycle to Ickleford there used to be a hermit living by the path on the right hand side. He had a beard and lived in a tin shack. He had an apple tree. We used to go birds nesting and collect sticklebacks from the stream at Walsworth down by the Sailor Boy. I liked to collect sticklebacks and keep them in a jam jar.

As a boy I lived in Haselfoot and in those days it wasn't built up - it was fields out in front of us where we played. We had a field behind us, which is now Icknield School, so that is where we used to spend our time. I have memories of our local gangs - nothing malicious, mind you. Haselfoot had their little gang and we used to go to see what Archers Way gang was getting up to. I remember digging in the field opposite where we lived in Archer's Way. Very sandy soil it must have been. We would dig these camps out. They were our little hide-aways. We did something very naughty too - we used to light spreader fires. Quite awful we were. We would pick a stretch of grass and set light to it. Terrible - I suppose it got the adrenaline flowing. I would think of it with horror now.

I remember as a boy a lot of my time in the holidays was spent in Haselfoot. I remember the old barn where the River Pix meandered through, eventually going into the Common and the old barn was where we played.

I can remember once doing something with Michael. He was one of the rougher kids on Jackmans Place. The family lived on the corner of the cul de sac. We did something we should not have done. There was a lorry left there. I don't remember whether Michael or I pulled the handbrake off. It was parked outside the garage doors and it rolled down and banged into the garage doors. We soon got out of there! In those days they were not so security conscious, there's no doubt

We had a village policeman such as it is. He came down from Yorkshire, lived in Letchworth years and years. Big tall copper, still about. He'd clump you round the ear-hole, or kick you up the backside, mate.

There were seasons for games - conker seasons, whips and tops, and one of the favourites was hoops made of three ply wood. They were light to spin and we spent hours running round the streets and bowling them along and chasing them all round town.

Talking of those cardboard tops reminds me of the first real prototype ice lolly - Snofrute from Wall's. It was in cardboard and it was triangular and you could push it up as you ate. You could push it further up. I think they were about a ha'penny. That was before the War. Directly the War started all things like Wall's all went, and then we never saw any ice cream really until after the War. First of all there were two brothers from Baldock, called the Jeffrey brothers. They used to come up with a motor bike and sidecar, and then Medlocks from Langford, they started up. But I remember also there was a shop during the War where round the back they had like a conservatory and we used to get on a bus and go on a Sunday and they used to make ice cream there, in Stotfold, right by the Green. I don't know the name. There was a bus service to Stotfold - not many, about two on a Sunday, but we used to get over there just solely to get an ice cream and come back. In those days we were easily pleased.

I remember going on steam trains. It was the workman's. To get a cheap ticket you got up at crack of dawn and went on what was called the workman's train. It was very early. We were not allowed to look out of the windows because we would get covered in soot. I do remember the steam trains, but I don't know when they were phased out. When I commuted some of these trains were still being used. If you were a woman travelling on your own it wasn't very nice in the non-corridor carriages. You would walk along to try to get in a corridor one.

Our third child went to the Nevells Road nursery school. My wife used to walk her there across the Common, taking the youngest, little Jill, in the pram. From the earliest Jill was determined to do everything that Claire, the older one, was allowed to do. So sometimes, when she was supposed to be playing on the green outside, she would slip away across Wilbury Road, make her way across the Common, stand by the gate to the playground until the children came out to play, and then go in with them. The teacher would ring us up and say, "She is here again". We thought it was a bind to have to go off and get her back, but we were not worried about her safety.

I left Newcastle in 1949 at the age of 14. The headmaster gave me all the references and so on and passed the word to me, "It's now about March time," he said, "your 15th birthday is in June. It is hardly worth going back to school, if you are moving down". So I took him at his word. We came down here, moved into Hallmead and of course I could not get a job. I was in-between age (14). So I was out the front in the street in Hallmead playing football on my own. A guy pulled up in a car. He said, "Aren't you at school?" So I said, "No". I said I had left school. He said "How old are you then?" I said, "14". He said, "What school do you go to?" I said I had just got down here from the North, Newcastle. I finished my school there and as I am 15 in June I need not go to school. He said where did I live? I said with my parents. He marched me across the road and knocked at the house. My mother came out. I said, "Here is a guy wants to talk to you". He was a School Inspector. He said, "Your son should be at school; he has a few months to go". The next thing I knew I got a letter and they shipped me off to Norton Road School from about March until the summer. That's when I left.

Children's games

When we first lived in Eastholm my boy George loved wild things and he got frog spawn and tadpoles and he used to take his lunch on his fairy cycle to that pond in Norton to get frog spawn in a medicine bottle and the tadpoles actually grew into frogs.

We went to the Common a lot. And to Radwell, because we used to go that way as well and down through the village and across the little footpath to the farm to Norton Bury and then along the stream to Radwell. We used to play a lot down there in summer holidays by the stream and Norton Bury.

I remember the Arena in the town - where they used to have the Fairs. And across from the Arena they had the Fire Station with a green fire engine! Then next door to that they had a very small Cinema - The Palace, the first purpose built Cinema in Britain. I can remember the Broadway opening as well. That was quite an occasion. I remember seeing "Snow White" there. That was the first time I ever went.

I remember going to the Circus where the Arena shops are now.

We used to play marbles all the way home, in the gutter and in the dirt bit. There was the path, then about six or eight feet of dirt before the houses, so we would often play marbles in those bits. We played marbles in Jackmans Place as well. I remember quarrelling with

Sylvia once. She reckoned I cheated. I managed to acquire a reasonable collection of marbles. I had a big tin in the indoor coal shed in Jackmans Place. There was competition in the playground and all the way home and in the rec. I used to sell them. It was 20 for an old penny, 10 for a ha'penny. Kids used to come and knock on the door, sometimes while I was having tea or something - "Can I have ten marbles?" The alleys - big glass ones - they were two-ers or four-ers. We had those, and coloured ones, and white and red ones and bloodshot ones.

In those days the grass in Jackmans Place rec. was covered with dandelions and hawkbits, flowers and butterflies everywhere, and bushes. We used to have a Tarzan tree down Dunhams Lane before they built up all the factories down there. We used to climb, but I never got very far. One or two got up very high. I was not one of the high climbers.

Cigarette cards were strong during the War. We used to take them to school, stand them up against the wall and flick them over and win them. It was one of our favourite games. Then we used to go round picking them up out of the fag packets people had thrown away. Sometimes men used to walk around picking up dog ends and roll their own cigarettes out of them. I used to take an old shoebox to school when I was at Pixmore and cut a hole in the side and stick cigarette cards round it and charge a couple of cards to look, or a farthing or a halfpenny to look - your own little cinema.

We used to play Chalk Chase. We would run around and go even to Weston sometimes. Someone used to go ahead drawing arrows, and you had to find them. They were supposed to do an arrow every twenty feet, or something. You gave them a quarter of an hour start and then several of you would go running round trying to find them.

There was a game played at the Grammar School where somebody stood with their back to the wall and someone put their head down between their legs, then you would try to pull them over or knock them off. People tried to pile up on one another and I never wanted to be under the pile. If they collapsed you said "Weak horses, weak horses" and you had to go again. Some would jump as far as they could and others try to pile on top. If you fell off sideways because the pile had got too big you would have to have a go underneath.

The Common

One of the best parts of my early childhood in Letchworth was the wonderful open Common with the Bandstand. I loved going through the Common as a shortcut when we were visiting relations and going to other parts of the town. We used to pick sloes and wild raspberries as we went through.

> NORTON COMMON BANDSTAND
> NEXT SUNDAY, 3 and 7.30 p.m.
> Letchworth Salvation Army Band
> Under the auspices of Letchworth Urban District Council

The Common had a bandstand then and a brass band gave concerts to people in deck chairs. You can still see traces of the bandstand's foundation if you look for them. There used to be lots and lots of children playing there in the fifties. The bridge over the stream was a favourite play place for children who, like my son, had an affinity for mud and water. East of the bridge the water comes from a pipe and it was a favoured occupation of the bold to crawl along this pipe until it came out near the swimming baths. The west side of the Common was then as wild as it is now, but the north-west looked out on a cornfield, the area that is now occupied by the houses of Hawthorn Hill and Wheat Hill.

We used to go to the Common a lot. When my mother went shopping with a friend she used to leave us to play in the Common - while they went to the shops. She would leave us with a picnic and some lemonade and we would play until they came and picked us up, perhaps an hour later. There was a bandstand in the middle - past the swimming pool. We used to play a lot in that dell, near the Glebe Road entrance to the Common. There was a big dip there. I presume something had been taken out of it, and we used to play a lot there, in that bit up to Wilbury Road from the back of Norton Way North. That was where we usually played and then they would pick us up on the way back home.

The Common was different then. I remember going by the stream which was much more wooded. You could walk through to the stile. I was never keen on going through the pipe under the road, although my friends did. I was not brave enough to do that. I remember falling in the water there once, in the paddling pool area of the stream. I got my trousers soaked. The water was dirty in those days. I got some illness or other and Mum blamed the dirty water.

I remember the band concerts that they used to have on the Common on the bandstand in the dip. The Town Band used to play on Sunday afternoons and evenings in the summer.

St Paul's Christmas Party

When I first moved into Letchworth, every Christmas time for years and years we used to go to the St Paul's Christmas party. It was absolutely fantastic, all the decorations and the balloons and the Christmas tree. They stopped it during the War or just after. When they stopped it we used to go to that little church at the corner of Spring Road and Broadwater Avenue.

Teenagers

As the children grew into teenagers they met in the town centre and in the 50s embraced rock and roll.

Saturday afternoons we all used to meet in the town - as teenagers do - just sit there giggling and talking to the boys as you do. There were a lot of people in Letchworth at that time. There were Italians, Polish people, Latvians. Some Hungarians came over too.

Rock 'n' roll was condemned across the nation and I embraced it enthusiastically, driving our poor neighbours to distraction with Elvis and Tommy Steele and 'Six Five Special' on Saturday nights. The aisles of the Palace Cinema were patrolled during the screening of 'Rock, Rock, Rock' and we did our best to promote an air of caveman depravity by shrieking and screaming but not smashing up the seats as we'd read about in the Daily Mirror.

Doctors and illness

Childhood of course was not all play; sometimes children were ill. An outbreak of scarlet fever meant schools were closed and those who caught the disease were moved to an isolation hospital.

Dr Rodger lived on Grange Road and held a surgery at his home on certain days which was very handy for young mothers.

We had medical inspections at school every year, and they used to test your hearing, and you had to bend over and touch your toes. I remember that at Wilbury School. Dr Kies was our doctor, and Dr Burgess. My father was from Edinburgh, and Dr Burgess was from Edinburgh too.

I am going back now to Westbury School in 1939-40. Our already large class of over 40 was augmented by London evacuees to well over 50. In 1940 May and June we had a Scarlet Fever epidemic which ran through the school like wild fire because we were all so tightly packed together in our desks. I caught Scarlet Fever in July of 1940 and the isolation hospital, which is now Rosehill Hospital, was full to over-flowing. I was taken by ambulance, because we had to be isolated. The Sanitary Inspector had to come to seal up the bedroom and fumigate the whole place. I was carted off to Baldock, to a house that was requisitioned from Sir Timothy Eden - Sir Anthony's brother - and that's where I ended up in hospital. When I got there a lot of people from Westbury School were there also. In fact there were more Letchworth children there than Baldock children. I got out of the hospital after a fortnight because I was an only child so I could recuperate at home. I was not allowed near any other children for several weeks. The week after I got out of the hospital a bomb fell behind the hospital at Baldock and people came knocking on my mother's door to say what had happened and they were going over there. My mother said, "It's alright, Greta's home" so that was another jolly event that happened.

I remember Norton Road School being quarantined for six weeks because there was an outbreak of Scarlet Fever. The classes were turned into dormitories. I was one of them because I had Scarlet Fever and so did my family and we weren't allowed to go home at all. We were all isolated.

Because the outbreak occurred at the School, the school itself was quarantined. They used it as a recuperation centre. There were doctors and nurses coming in every day to check the kids - and some of the teachers had to be there as well. That was six weeks, I remember that. During that time there was always air raids going on as well. The sirens kept going off. It was a funny sort of situation but you made the most of it because you had to. There was no such thing as you didn't want to - you did it.

I remember one summer my sister was taken ill with Scarlet Fever, our Doctor was Dr Craggs from the Norton Way surgery. He came and said that she had to go to an isolation hospital. The ambulance came and I waved her goodbye, as a man sealed the bedroom door with tape, after lighting a sulphur candle to fumigate the room. I had slept in the same bedroom with my sister, so as Dr Cragg was afraid I might be incubating the disease, he had me moved to another room at home. He said I had to be isolated from my friends for a few weeks, until he was absolutely sure I was all right. These were mostly long hot days and as I was on my own time hung heavy. At the back of our long garden there was a long spinney, the whole length of our road with a big open space before the farmland beyond. This open space eventually became the prefab development of Bedford Road, but at this time it was a huge meadow left fallow and consequently full of wild flowers, butterflies and all manner of insects. So I passed the time making a wildlife book full of drawings of everything I saw. I would look them up in our big heavy set of encyclopaedias and label them accordingly. Although I missed school and my friends, I was getting some sort of education during this period. It was marvellous to be in a wide open space, free to do as I pleased, even though I wasn't allowed to mix with other children; part of the Garden City ethos that certainly worked for me at that time.

We did visit my sister but I had to sit in the rose garden on a wooden bench, so I could wave to her at a window whilst my mother was inside. The isolation hospital was actually South Lodge in Baldock, since then a school. My sister recovered completely and eventually came home.

Very early in the War, maybe the War had not quite started, my young brother was in the hospital, and the Matron said there was nothing she could do any more, would we take him home, because they had got orders to clear the hospitals out for anybody coming home from the War wounded. This they did; the hospital was cleared, but it never came to that at that time.

I can remember when I was a kid; the period when I went from Hillshott to Pixmore was when I caught scarlet fever. I was sent home from class because I was developing a rash and feeling sick, and so mum had to get the doctor. I had got scarlet fever, so they took me to the isolation hospital on top of Letchworth Hill on the Hitchin road (Rosehill now). I remember my parents had to come and see me behind a glass window.

MOLLIE LANGFORD

A.I.S.T.D., B.B., S.B Highly Commended

School of Dancing

"THE STUDIO"   COMMERCE LANE
LETCHWORTH

ALL BRANCHES TAUGHT   CHILDREN AND ADULTS
Ballroom, Tap, Ballet, Musical Comedy
PRIVATE LESSONS, 10 a.m.—10 p.m.

★ In the event of callers finding the Studio closed a written inquiry will be answered by return of post

---

15 Schools

In the period from 1939 to 1960 schooling in Letchworth changed, with evacuees filling the schools during the War and the building of new schools afterwards.

Wartime schooling

The War meant that changes had to be made in schools. Classes were very large because of the number of evacuee children who had to be accommodated. Some subjects had to be stopped – domestic science being one of these due to rationing.

School routine continued with some modifications. We no longer had a gym or domestic science department - my first form room in Letchworth had been the Grammar School domestic science room with sinks and cupboards surrounding our desks. Girls who were taking the subject at a higher level did their practical work at Pixmore School. Our school dinners were provided at St. Francis College and war-time shortages led to Grammar School pupils attending some of our Latin classes and the sharing of certain English Literature set books with Letchworth School Certificate candidates.

I used to absolutely love the maypole dancing. We did a lot of country dancing anyway in school all the year round. Don't think we did a lot of P.E. We did drill in the yard in lines, but we didn't play games. We didn't do netball or football or anything like that as they do now. We did drill and we did country dancing. We had singing each week and we had a percussion band that we used to do. So really we had quite a good curriculum. I remember also we did knitting for the troops in our sewing lessons when we were in the top class, 11. We knitted balaclava helmets and mittens and knitted in airforce blue. I think the wool was sent to the school in batches and I dread to think what some of the articles were like when they were finished. Whether they were of any use or not I don't know.

When I was at the Grammar School there wasn't any cookery until after the war because, of course, part of that was used by evacuees as well. Bexhill School used part of the Grammar School. We didn't do anything except really academic subjects until after the War. There was no sewing. Although we did do sewing at Norton - aprons and hankies and things like that. I think as rationing got tighter those sort of things - we had not got the material or things for cookery.

Girls of St Vincent House, St Francis College 1940/41

When I got to St. Francis we were full to the rafters with European refugees, only girls and women I hasten to add. All the men, if they had left home, were billeted out in the town because being a full-blown Convent in those days we could only take girls and women. There was a building built for a school I think from the South Coast - I think from Bexhill - so they did their school work there. We had to go to school dead on time at nine o'clock. I remember being up three nights with air-raid warnings wailing all the time and I had to go and sit in the cupboard under the stairs. I was very tired one night and I thought I would do my homework when the raids were on. I got to school next day - nothing had happened that night, and I had not done my homework, so I scribbled a bit of it before Assembly. But I got into terrible trouble from one of the Sisters who said that Mr Hitler had beaten me because he had got me down so much I had not been able to do my homework. After that I can tell you that Mr Hitler did not beat me any more. I always made sure I did everything. But we did have some very disturbed nights but, luckily, no tragedies in Letchworth.

After the war ended rationing continued and even school children had to do their bit for the "war effort". Pupils from local schools went potato picking.

We were sent potato picking to a farm from school and it was extremely hard work for twelve year olds. We climbed into lorries as we arrived at school in the morning, weighed down with wellingtons and our packed lunch, and were driven to a farm (probably the other side of Stotfold). On being allocated to a field we were issued with buckets and as the tractor travelled up and down the strips of land, lifting the potatoes, we had to collect them and load them on to a cart. We were extremely cold and wet by the end of the day when we were taken back to school. This was our "war effort" for which we were paid the princely sum of five shillings a week (25p). The hot mug of cocoa served to us during the morning was most welcome, but I remember having to work extremely fast to finish picking potatoes from one row before the tractor arrived again having lifted yet another load!

Our class at Letchworth Grammar School was asked to go potato picking on local farms because many men were not yet demobilised. We called it "spud bashing" and we loved it, getting out of lessons, going off every day for a week in an open lorry, singing songs at the tops of our voices. We worked hard gathering the potatoes all day and we ate our sandwiches sitting on straw bales, drinking strong cocoa from the van which came round the fields regularly.

It's milk time for these young pupils at Hillshott School in 1945

Primary Schools

I don't think many of the schools had nursery classes at that time. I worked at Hillshott for a while and I think they were one of the first schools to have a nursery class because they were the first school to have a lot of children from India and Pakistan as a lot of people went to live in that area. Also there were a lot of Hungarians, Poles, and I think to help the children get a good language development before they started school. I think that was one of the first schools to open a nursery and to help the children with their language development before they started their formal teaching. It was a very good school.

At Hillshott I remember my teachers Miss Couthard, Miss Barton, Miss Grey and Miss Leighton. Miss Primett was Headmistress.

I went to school at Hillshott School during the latter part of the War. I can remember as soon as an air raid was coming on we would have to go down stairs in an inner part of the school and sit there until the all clear went. The biggest thing I remember is at lunch time we used to go to lunch and we used to march down the road to the old Free Church hall and there was always a rush to get to the front because the front ones carried the milk bottles. As we walked down Hillshott so we used these like cymbals, banging in step as we walked down to the Free Church hall. We had our lunch there then came back. In the latter twelve months of my school time there they actually built a portable canteen there, so we ended up having meals at the school itself.

When I left Hillshott I went up to Pixmore School. Of the particular teachers I remember, Miss Carlisle was an old Letchworthian, and

SCHOOLS 157

Pixmore School

Dance display 1951

Sports Day 1952

The 1946 1st Form

The school football team in 1947

Miss Lake. They were the R.I. (religious instruction) teachers. There was a Mr Houghton, who was about six foot eight. He used to give you his size eleven slipper across your backside. The other chap I remember was Willy Walters. He used to use a swordstick, or grab hold of your hair and rub your knuckles into your hair if you did anything naughty. He would come along behind you with his swordstick, hold your hand on your head and whack your backside. The Headmaster at that time was a Mr Borer, who lived out at Ashwell.

I went to Westbury School for my infants and juniors, so that was from aged five to 11, from 1942 to 1947-ish. One of my earliest memories was when I was in the infants' part. The Headmistress of the infants' was Miss Cutler. I remember a big heap of raffia mats that we used to get out in the afternoon to have a lay down, as it was required that we should have a sleep. I think this was required at Hillshott as well.

The Headmistress of the junior part was a Miss Virgin who was very strict. Looked strict, sounded strict, was strict. We did not have a school canteen in those days so I can remember us 'crocodiling' up to St. Francis' College sometimes and other times down to the Church Rooms. I can remember we used to go off about 12 o'clock for school dinners. Eventually they were at Westbury but I can remember Miss Virgin and Miss Cutler were the two Heads. I can remember the rap on the knuckles with the ruler was very painful. Miss Virgin ruled the roost.

Westbury Nursery Class 1958

My first memories of Westbury were of playing with sand and water in bowls on a table, bottles of milk in crates in a corner of the classroom and having to go to the outside toilets across the playground, down in a dip, near the bottom gate of the school.

Westbury was a cold, forbidding place in my first winter term, I had to wear a liberty bodice and thick tights to keep warm. We often had snow and frost on the playground; the toilets froze, also the cardboard tops on the milk bottles were perched on two or three inches of frozen milk. I remember after school lunch, we had to lie down on little grass mats, placed around the parquet floor of the hall, to have a rest or sleep, whilst Miss Green, Miss Thomas, Miss Howard or Miss Virgin, the Headmistress kept a watchful eye on us.

The Grange School opened in October 1951 and initially taught five to eleven year olds. In 1957 Northfields Infants School was completed, taking the five to seven year olds and leaving the Grange as a Junior School.

In 1949 I had joined the staff of Norton Road Junior and Infants School under the Headship of Mr Bob Unstead of "Looking at History" fame. I remember doing dinner duty in the Norton Methodist building in Common View until the Grange estate was developed and the whole school moved into the new Grange Junior and Infants building out in the fields in 1951. We were there before the houses were built, surrounded by grass and wild flowers, with larks and bees outside the lovely light glass windows of this modern

Westbury Infants School Nativity Play 1959

building. Once a pupil found a leveret crouched in the grass outside our classroom. In 1952 the conductor Sir Adrian Boult, officially opened the school, but I left this paradise in 1953.

The classes were quite large then. They were all 40 to 45 in those times. The school had about 500 children. We used to have 120 in a year. We used to have four lots of 30 at the bottom and all the rest of the way through the junior school it was three lots of 40. We also had odd little classes which were remedial classes and others as well. The first class I went back to take full-time, that was 45. They went down gradually to 40.

Before they opened Wilbury School we used to have children come to the Grange by coach from that area. Two coaches every day used to bring children to the Grange. The first flats they built in Icknield Way were all for families and, of course, they were so crowded because they were only one or two bedroom flats but they all had to have families to get them because housing was so difficult. Then when they started building the Grange houses a lot of those families later transferred on to the Grange into bigger houses. In the meanwhile they were waiting for Wilbury School to be built they were using Simmonds Coaches to bring the children each day - quite little children, infants as well as juniors. Gradually then they went to Wilbury School and then we had them back again when they transferred to the Grange for bigger houses.

Anne Dixon assists these young pupils at the opening of the Grange Branch Public Library - Junior section, 1957

I started at the Grange School when I was five years old, in 1956. Northfields Infants' school hadn't been finished then, so the infants and juniors were in the same school. We moved to Northfields the following year when it was finished, and then I moved back to the Grange Junior School when I was seven. The first day at school everyone started at a different time and my friend Susan had started earlier than I did. When I got there she was playing with the sand, so when the teacher asked me what I wanted to do I said I wanted to play with the sand as well.

I remember three teachers in particular at the Grange. Mr Gay was the Headmaster and there were Miss Golding and Miss Fitzpatrick. Miss Golding was very strict, but in retrospect I can see she was a very good teacher.

We used to have individual school photos taken, and they sat us in front of a mural in the entrance hall for it. The mural depicted longboats and they positioned us so that we had a boat coming out of either side of our head. We had to sit at a table with our arms crossed.

I was part of the post war baby boom. Consequently I went to the Grange School by coach from Bedford Road. The headmaster was R. J. Unstead who wrote those history textbooks for Junior Schools in the 50s and 60s. The newly opened Wilbury School (1949) was bursting at the seams and the infants had overflowed into St Thomas Church Hall, Bedford Road. I went there two terms later. There were two classes, separated by a curtain. The floor was very dusty and the paint was a dull sea green. Miss Haws had the younger children and Miss Fitzpatrick taught the older infants.

I remember my time at Wilbury School clearly. Teaching was quite regulated and formal with tables, spellings and sitting in desks of 2. Mr Smith was the Headmaster and his wife taught the young juniors. The most enlightened teacher was Mr Golightly. With him we had debates and mock elections. There was also Mrs Skinner and her aunt Miss Coulthard. The Deputy Head Mr Horton later became Headmaster of Graveley School.

We were constantly reminded that our goal was to pass the '11 plus' exam!

"CHILDREN WILL COME HERE WITH PLEASURE"
Opening of Wilbury Primary School

Secondary Schools

At 11 years of age pupils sat the 11 Plus examination which decided whether they would go to the Grammar School or the Secondary. The only Secondary school in Letchworth at that time was Norton. The examination and the interview that went with it is still remembered by those who took part in the process.

Most children went to Letchworth Grammar School or Norton Secondary Modern School (as they were then known) A few of us caught the bus to the Hitchin Grammar School every day.

When we moved onto the Grange the children went to the local schools there, and then they progressed to the Grammar School. Grange School was a good school; Mr Gay was a very nice man, very keen on rugby. The Norton Road School featured a lot. Two of the girls went there. The oldest daughter passed the eleven-plus but she had to go to Norton because there were not enough places at the Grammar School. She was in the bumper year. It would have been 1957-58. She had to go to Norton then transfer to do the senior school at the Grammar School. I liked the Grammar School. My second daughter went straight to the Grammar School because things had changed slightly and there were not so many children.

The main Grammar School headmaster in my time was Mr Wilkinson. Miss Exton was there, "Tiggy" McBride, Mr Marsden. Mr Clark was a PT instructor. He used to bang people's heads together to shut them up. I never wanted my head cracked in. "Tiggy" McBride was Geography and Maths. Miss Carter was Deputy Head or one of the senior teachers. She had a long run. The War changed the appearance of the school. They had nice brown paper strips all over the windows. There was an air raid shelter across the road in the gardens, but I don't recall going down it. I can't recall any particular changes in the school. I never got bombed or anything. The playing fields had a back entrance in Broadwater Avenue between the houses. You went to Spring Road. I didn't like cross country so I half walked round Roxley Court. In the end I got letters from my mum saying I was not very strong, I had a cold, so I had to pick up dandelions and dig them out of the rugby pitch and the football pitch in the games lessons.

I cycled to school at the Grammar School. I would cycle up Gernon Road. I previously went to Hillshott until I was 11, took my 11-plus and then went to the Grammar School. I remember getting my letter to say I had passed and I got quite upset because I thought my friends possibly would not be going, but I felt quite happy when I got to school and found out that some of my friends were going so that was quite nice. Cycling up Gernon Road when I got to the top I could chose which way I was going around the Town Square - I could either go right or left as there were no one-way system in those days. So it was quite pleasant in those days cycling.

When I was still at school we went up to London by train to the Dome of Discovery. I can remember the Grammar School and different events. I remember being sent to the Headmaster and standing under the clock. I can remember taking the 11-plus one Saturday morning. We sat the theory side at our own school but the written part was at the Grammar School. He was a good old-fashioned Headmaster, like the film of Mr. Chips. He wore spats and his gown flowing. If ever there was a class where the teacher wasn't there he would come and teach algebra which was his pet subject. I was at the Grammar School for a few years, until I was about 15 and a half.

At this time I had just passed the 11-plus and left the nearby Norton Road School to attend Letchworth Grammar School in the Broadway. My parents were able to obtain the obligatory school uniform at Spink's in Leys Avenue, which included a Panama hat for the summer and felt hat for the winter, complete with elastic chin-strap.

We had school uniform at the Grammar School. They were quite strict. There was a certain day when you went into summer uniform and a certain day when you went into winter uniform, with the navy tunics. We had to wear short socks, and it was cold! Miss Carter, the Deputy Head decreed you had to wear ankle socks. We were not allowed to wear stockings, even though it was cold. We had to wear berets. If you were seen without them you were in trouble. We tried to wear them in, so they were not so pristine. I used to cycle to school and come home to lunch. School meals had a terrible reputation; that was probably why I used to go home!

Mr Lill was there (at the Grammar School). There were three houses, Neville, which I was in, Howard and Gorst. I think Gorst was green and Neville was blue. You were in houses mainly for the sports. I remember Mary. Mary was a prefect when I was there.

You did the 11-plus, then if you passed the exam you went for an interview. Mr Lill was the one who did my interview. He did not believe in corporal punishment. You had to stay in and write lines if you made a mistake. We played hockey and tennis. We used to have to go in our shorts along Broadwater Avenue and Spring Road and up to the playing fields. We used to go up the back gate. If the weather was bad we had to do cross country running - awful! We used to have to go down towards Willian, because it was not built on then. Oh, it was dreadful! I remember getting stuck in the mud. I didn't enjoy it. It was a big circuit, really.

I had to take some intelligence tests at school and an 11-plus exam, which I remember doing sitting in the hall of Westbury School. The time came for me to follow up with an interview at the Grammar School in Broadway, opposite the Rose Gardens. I was really nervous as I sat outside the headmaster's door waiting for my turn. I was summoned into Mr Wilkinson's office by Miss Cundell to find him sitting there in his gown and mortar board. He looked so friendly with his white hair and moustache, a real grandfather face and twinkle in his eye. My actual interview consisted of him saying, "I hear you're good at drawing. Draw me". By the time he had turned sideways in a pose the paper and pencil had already been provided, so I drew him. I was then accepted into the Grammar School.

Letchworth Grammar School was another milestone in my life, a very happy time. I thrived on it all and made lots of new friends. Some came in by train and bus from Baldock, Ashwell and Royston. My father's family had all come from the Ashwell and Royston area so he was delighted that I made many friends from the area. He would often know the whole family and history of these friends, and would recall playing with their fathers.

The Grammar School used the playing fields behind the houses in Spring Road for games and athletics. We used to have to walk crocodile fashion backwards and forwards, whatever the weather to our sports lessons.

Before the Grange School was built, primary age pupils had been at Norton Road School along with the secondary pupils.

I came to teach at Norton Road School, as it was then called, in 1949. At that time the only state schools for secondary pupils were Norton Road, Pixmore School and the Grammar School. St. Christopher was a progressive private school with a Quaker head, Mr. Lyn Harris, and St. Francis was a Catholic school for girls.

The Head Teacher of Norton Road School, the Headmaster as they were then called, was Mr Haysman, known as Jimmy Haysman to everybody - a dedicated, much loved colleague. By the time I joined it, the school had lost its wartime evacuees, but the classes still hovered on the forty to a class mark. Heaven knows how they managed during the War. They were fortunate in possessing several teachers of sterling worth of the old school: Mr 'Dicky' Dykes the Deputy Head, Mrs Jepson, Mr West, the woodwork teacher and a young graduate (one of a small minority in those days), Miss Hardy who taught English literature and was about the same age as we ex-servicemen. Some oddities from the war years remained with us. A half-acre of the school playing field had been 'dug for victory' and we kept this going in the early post-war years, for rationing continued and our crops helped the school kitchen. We also lost the railings that had separated the boys' and girls' playgrounds. To the surprise of some of the traditionalists, this made no difference at all.

The greatest change and challenge for the post-war school was that under the new Labour government the old elementary schools, with children from five to fourteen, had just been split into junior schools for the under elevens and secondary schools for the older children. The two schools now shared the building, but with goodwill and two excellent head teachers all went smoothly. The head of the new Norton Road Juniors was Mr Bob Unstead, an energetic, intelligent teacher ideally suited for the new world of post-war education. He had already made his name by the publication of what was probably the first book for junior school children, a history of England, whose style and language were appropriate for the new educational climate. It sold throughout England and Wales and was soon followed by further equally excellent books dealing with other school subjects.

As the Grange Estate grew the juniors left us and moved into the newly-built Grange Juniors. Later Mr Unstead left teaching and joined Blacks, the publishers, as head of their school books department.

It was soon time for Mr Haysman to retire, now that he had seen the school through the war years. We had expected that Mr Dykes, the Deputy Head, would take his place but he realised that in the new world of secondary schools he was unlikely to get a headship without a degree, so he applied for and received the headship of Hillshott Juniors.

Our new head was Mr Edgar John, an intelligent, longsighted, able administrator, well suited to lead a secondary school into the future. As a good Welshman he introduced rugby, but we were unable to sustain this, as there were no schools we could play against. A more challenging issue was the raising of the school leaving age. It had been raised to 15 a few years before and was now 16 years of age. At first, schools taught an expanded version of the old five to 14 syllabus but the new two years of schooling called for new thinking. During this period an even hotter subject of discussion, for teachers and parents alike, was the 11-plus exam. Towards the end of their last year in the junior school, children were now set exams in English and mathematics and an intelligence test. From these, the twenty five percent of children who succeeded were deemed suitable for the Grammar School and the remainder deemed suitable for the secondary moderns. The Grammar School children would follow a syllabus which enabled them to take exams which would lead on to higher education, the secondary children would not. Mr John thought it not right that secondary children should be excluded from these chances and began to make it possible for the most able of the Norton Road children to take the higher exams. He was one of the first secondary modern head teachers in England to do this. In a sense, Mr. John was anticipating the creation of the comprehensive school.

Whilst developing the new curriculum, he maintained some of our traditional activities. The children still elected the May Queen and we carried on the enormously popular May Day celebrations with maypole dancing and the older classes taking their turn to do country dances. The boys were as keen on this as were the girls. One year it poured

CROWNED QUEEN OF MAY | Fortieth Norton May Day festival

Crowning of The May Queen at Norton Road School's 1st post war May Day 1945.
(Pamela Iley, the 1944 Queen, crowns the new Queen, Freda Bates).

with rain. Normally each group performed a couple of dances and then came back into the school for a break before going on again to do another couple. This year, when the children returned sopping wet, we did not allow them to return into the rain. The boys were furious. I particularly recall our music master, Mr Gale, playing the piano in the downpour until the water made the keys stick, when another piano would be dragged out for him. He used up three pianos that day.

Mr. John took account of the extra year at school by introducing a secretarial course for girls, with typing and shorthand, and had set up a metalwork workshop for the boys. This enabled many boys to gain engineering skills which helped them to be accepted for apprenticeships in the many engineering enterprises in the Letchworth of the fifties.

Twenty boys were also able to go to the county's camp at Cuffley, accompanied by myself and another member of staff. The camp was another Hertfordshire 'first'. School camps were not new, but previously they were hutted accommodations. Cuffley was the first permanent county camp in tents. Having two teachers away from school made a staff shortage, so in a subsequent year I took them on my own. This still caused the children to miss a week's normal lessons, so in subsequent years I took the children during the Whitsun half-term holiday.

I also set up a boxing club as an evening out-of-school activity. It was very popular and we won many county championships. Each year I took the county champions to the sports centre of the British Oxygen Company in Edmonton, where the Schools' A.B.A. held their quarter finals for the British Schoolboy Boxing Championships.

I remember Miss Clark. She was our biology teacher and she did nature studies as well. She was quite a woman, she was. A lot of people disliked her intensely but I think the thing was you had to know her. Once she got to know you she was quite a girl. I really did like her. She was a woman I could respect even from a child's point of view. I didn't dislike her. There was another teacher there, Miss Harding. She was a music teacher. There was Mr. Betts - he was an art teacher- Mr. James and Mr. Farrar - he came from Eastholm Green.

I remember the maypole dancing and the boys used to do sword dancing It was really quite a good show. The parents were there, surrounding the field. It was really quite a thing. The flowers were gorgeous. One time they used to have an accordionist. After that they had somebody playing the piano over loud speakers but that was good and somehow or other they always seemed to have a nice day for it. It was very rarely it was washed out. They were gorgeous days.

I was living in Hallmead at that time. We used to walk across the fields to get to school. There used to be a path that ran right round St Thomas à Becket Church in Bedford Road. We used to go right down there to the River Pix, across a couple of meadows, and up I think it is called Wheathill now - or Hawthorn Hill - then we used to cut through the Common and then we would get to the school that way. We always went to school that way, day and night. It was nearly a two-mile walk really. It was quite a walk.

Norton Road School May Day 1945

I was at Norton Road Primary School from 1944 to 1950 when I left to go to Hitchin Boys' Grammar School and the Headmaster latterly was R.J. Unstead - Bob Unstead - who became the Head at the Grange Junior School when that opened in 1951. I can remember him saying to us that he thought history books were totally boring and that he was going to write history books that were of interest to children with not so much text but more pictures. Subsequently, he did leave teaching and he was involved with the publishers and millions of his history books were published not only in this country but throughout the world in different languages.

I can remember also getting up there as early as I could in the morning because the milkman would be delivering the milk and it was a horse-drawn milk float, and if I was lucky I would get there when he was just delivering down at the primary end. Then there would be a ride on the milk float round to the senior end of the school.

Then, our playing field bordered on what is now the Grange Estate. When you stood on the fence of the playing field you would look out over the fields towards Stotfold and on a clear day you could see the barrage balloons over Cardington. I can remember the building work starting, I think in 1947, with the houses in Eastern Way and, of course, it took off from there.